Five Who Changed the World

Other books authored or
edited by Daniel Akin:

.

A Theology for the Church

God on Sex

1, 2, 3 John (in NAC)

Song of Songs (in HOTC)

Discovering the Biblical Jesus

The Believer's Study Bible

FIVE

WHO CHANGED THE WORLD

DANIEL L. AKIN

SOUTHEASTERN
BAPTIST THEOLOGICAL SEMINARY

Wake Forest, North Carolina

Five Who Changed the World

Copyright © 2008 by Daniel L. Akin and Southeastern Baptist Theological Seminary

Published by Southeastern Baptist Theological Seminary
        PO Box 1889
        Wake Forest, NC 27588

Cover photo: iStockPhoto

Printed in the United States of America.

This book is dedicated to Southeastern's International Church Planting students, who change the world every day.

Contents

Foreword

૪

Missions matters because God is a missionary God. Therefore, His people must be a missionary people. From Genesis to Revelation, we see God's central promise that He will send Messiah, and that Messiah will win the nations unto himself. It is through Messiah that God's glory will cover the earth. It is through Messiah that the lost will be saved.

And yet there are almost 2 billion people who have little or no access to Messiah. In many corners of the globe there are no churches, no Bibles, and no Christians to bear testimony. Many of these 2 billion people could leave their homes and search — for days and weeks and months — and never find a Christian, a Bible, or a church. It is our responsibility to remedy this. Our Lord commands us in Matthew 28: 18-20 to make disciples of *all* nations.

The magnitude of this task is great, but it is matched and exceeded by the magnitude of our biblical convictions: That God is a missionary God; that all people without Christ are lost; that a central theme in the Scriptures is God's desire to win the nations unto Himself; that since the coming of His Son, God has chosen that all saving faith be consciously focused on Christ; that the church's task in each generation is to proclaim the gospel to her generation; and that this progress of the gospel to the ends of the earth may be hindered temporarily, but there can be no doubt about its final triumph.

In Revelation 5, our Lord gives John a breathtaking vision. In this vision, all of heaven bursts forth into praise. Among those worshiping, John sees men and women from every tribe, tongue, people, and nation. This is the vision that drives us—that our Lord will be worshiped from all corners of the globe. He alone is worthy of such worship. Our lives should be lived in such a way as to contribute to this triumphant march of God, as He draws unto himself worshipers from every tribe, tongue, people, and nation.

This is the driving passion behind this series of missions messages preached by Danny Akin and collected in this book. In each message, he couples a passage of Scripture with a missionary biography. As he preaches through Matthew 28:16-20, Romans 8:28-39, Philippians 1:21, Romans 12:1, and Psalm 96, he expounds and illustrates those same passages with riveting lessons and stories from the lives of William Carey, Adoniram Judson, William Wallace, Lottie Moon, and Jim Elliot.

Be forewarned, however. This is a book for those who like their coffee strong. Those who read these messages will find themselves informed, rebuked, challenged, and motivated. They may even find themselves able to say, as Jim Elliot does in the pages of this book, that "He is no fool who gives what he cannot keep to gain that which he cannot lose."

Bruce R. Ashford
Director
Lewis A. Drummond Center for Great Commission Studies
Southeastern Baptist Theological Seminary
Wake Forest, N.C.

Introduction

❧

Several years ago the Lord showed me a wonderful truth in His Word. I discovered that the greatest missionary who ever lived was also the greatest theologian who ever lived. His name was Jesus. Upon further reflection the Lord pointed me to another truth that complemented this one. The greatest Christian missionary who ever lived was also the greatest Christian theologian who ever lived. His name was Paul. In fact, Paul was a missionary even before he began to excel as a writing theologian. I saw that the Bible reveals that there is no contradiction, no opposition, between the task of the theologian and the mandate of being a missionary. The two naturally go together!

It was out of this study in the Scriptures that God began to do a new work in my heart in the spring and summer of 2007. I had always known the value of reading Christian biography, but during that time I became particularly interested in Christian missionary biography. Further, Southeastern Baptist Theological Seminary has been known for a number of years as a Great Commission Seminary, but I felt impressed that the time had come to raise the bar and press the issue with an even greater intensity and sense of urgency. So, I began reading the biographies of William Carey, Adoniram Judson, Bill Wallace, Lottie Moon and Jim Elliot. I must say that both an admiration for these heroes's of the faith and a suffocating conviction gripped my soul. I rejoiced and I wept. And, I became convinced that our students, faculty and staff at Southeastern needed to know about these champions for Christ as well.

Because I am so deeply committed to Biblical Exposition, I had the idea of wedding, in a series of five sermons, the lives of these great missionaries and an appropriate Biblical text. William Carey is "the father" of the modern missionary movement, and so the Great Commission text of Matthew 28:16-20 was perfect. Adoniram Judson and his wife Ann (whom he called Nancy) were the first Baptist missionaries from America. Their lives were filled with such trials and sorrows that Romans 8:28-39 seemed especially fitting. Bill Wallace was a layman and a wonderful medical missionary who was brutally murdered by the Communist in China. On his grave marker those who loved him placed Philippians 1:21. That single verse beautifully summarizes this precious man's service to the Lord Jesus. Of course no one's name is better known among Southern Baptist than that of Lottie Moon, even if we know very little about her! Like Bill Wallace she never married, and like Dr. Wallace, she too served in China, literally killing herself in her love for our Savior and the Chinese people. Romans 12:1 is written all over her life. Finally I read the journal of Jim Elliot and other works about him by his wife Elizabeth Elliot. Like Bill Wallace, he determined to be a missionary as a teenager. Like Bill Wallace he was martyred for King Jesus. Jim Elliot was passionate to see the nations reached with the gospel. Psalm 96, one of the great missionary psalms, seemed to capture so beautifully his heart.

This is how these messages came into existence. The audio versions can be located at *www.danielakin.com* under the heading "Five Missionaries Who Changed The World." They can be downloaded at no cost. These five studies have greatly changed and impacted my own life. It is my prayer that our Lord might use them to encourage, convict and challenge his church to tell the world of a Savior who saves whose name is Jesus, and of a God who "is great and greatly to be praised" (Psalm 96:4).

Daniel Akin
President
Southeastern Baptist Theological Seminary
Wake Forest, N.C.

The Great Commission & William Carey: A Passionate Global Vision

ॐ

Matthew 28:16-20

William Carey may have been the greatest missionary since the time of the apostles. He rightly deserves the honor of being known as "the father of the modern missions movement." Carey was born in 1761, and he left England in 1793 as a missionary to India. He would never return home again, instead dying in 1834 among the people he had given his life to.

William Carey was poor, with only a grammar school education, and yet he would translate the Bible into dozens of languages and dialects. He established schools and mission stations all over India.

Timothy George (dean of Beeson Divinity School) described Carey as a "lone, little man. His resume would have read: Education – minimal. Degrees – none. Savings – depleted. Political influence – nil. References - a band of country preachers half a world away. What were Carey's resources? Weapon – love. Desire - to bring the light of God into the darkness. Strategy - to proclaim by life, lips, and letters the unsearchable riches of Christ" (Timothy George, *Faithful Witness,* 93).

William Carey understood Matthew 28:16-20. It was his farewell text to his church at Harvey Lane before departing to India. Though he had been rebuked earlier by the respected minister John Ryland Sr., Carey was undeterred. Ryland had told him, with his now infamous words, "Young man, sit down. When God pleases to convert the heathen, He will do without your aid or mine" (George, 53). Despite this, he would powerfully proclaim, "Expect great things. Attempt great things." (Later tradition would add "from God" and "for God" (George, 32), though this is undoubtedly what he meant).

He would publish his famous *An Enquiry into the Obligations of Christians to Use Means for the Conversion of the Heathens.* Here he would pen searing words for the church of his day, as well as our own. Commenting on the Great Commission text, found in Matthew 28:16-20, Carey wrote:

> This commission was as extensive as possible, and laid them under obligation to disperse themselves into every country to the habitable globe, and preach to all the inhabitants, without exception, or limitation. They accordingly went forth in obedience to the command, and the power of God evidently wrought with them. Many attempts of the same kind have been made since their day, and which have been attended with various success; but the work has not been taken up, or prosecuted of late years (except by a few individuals) with that zeal and perseverance with which the primitive Christians went about it. It seems as if many thought the commission

6

was sufficiently put in execution by what the apostles and others have done; that we have enough to do to attend to the salvation of our own countrymen; and that, if God intends the salvation of the heathen, he will some way or other bring them to the gospel, or the gospel to them. It is thus that multitudes sit at ease, and give themselves no concern about the far greater part of their fellow sinners, who to this day, are lost in ignorance and idolatry. (Sec. 1)

Carey would later add, "I question whether all are justified in staying here, while so many are perishing without means of grace in other lands" (Sec. 50).

The words found in Matthew 28 constitute the last words of Jesus in this gospel. They are intended to be lasting words and the final marching orders for Christ's followers until He returns. Adrian Rogers said here we find "the heartbeat of the Son of God." Here we are told that, "We are all to bring all men by all means to Jesus by any cost."

Acknowledge He Has All Power
Matthew 28:16-18

The eleven disciples minus Judas go north to Galilee "to the mountain where Jesus had told them to go" (NIV). The scene is reminiscent of the setting of the Sermon on the Mount (Matthew 5:1). It is interesting to note that the climatic temptation (Matt 4:8-11), the Sermon on the Mount (Matthew 5-7), the Transfiguration (Matthew 17:1), the Olivet Discourse prophecy (Matthew 24-25) and now the Great Commission of the Great King all took place on a mountain.

Suddenly they see the resurrected, risen Lord. What transpires is instructive for our careful consideration and response.

Worship Him, Matthew 28:17

Seeing Him the people worship. Amazingly though, some still doubt. Did they have doubts as to whether or not they should worship this man? Perhaps. Were their doubts confusion about the whole thing? Perhaps. Did the people doubt because they did not know how to respond given their past failures and track record? Almost certainly.

Even in the midst of their doubts, worship is the wise and right thing to do. Even when I may not understand all he is doing in my life, *worship*. If I am confused, unsure and hesitating, *worship*. When I am sorrowful, heart broken and crushed, *worship*. Am I discouraged, depressed and in utter despair? *Worship.* Even when I am at death's door? *Worship*!

On his deathbed, Carey breathed to the Scottish missionary Alexander Duff, "When I am gone, say nothing about Dr. Carey. Speak about Dr. Carey's Savior" (George, xii). Jesus is the Savior, so worship Him.

Hear Him, Matthew 28:18

"All (this word is used four times) authority is mine, in heaven and on earth."

Satan offered Him an earthly kingdom, but His Father planned so much more (Matt. 4:8-11). The words echo the great Son of Man text (Daniel 7:14) where the Bible declares of this heavenly, divine Man, "Then to Him was given dominion and glory and a kingdom, that all peoples, nations, and languages should serve Him. His dominion is an everlasting dominion, which shall not pass away, and His kingdom the one which shall not be destroyed" (NKJV). John Piper gets to the heart of these words and says,

> Here we see the *peak of power*. Notice verse 18. Jesus says, 'All authority in heaven and on earth has been given to me.' If you gathered all the authority of all the governments and armies of the world and put them in the scales with the authority of the risen Christ, they would go up in the balance like air. *All authority* on earth has been given to the risen Christ. *All* of it! The risen Christ has the right to tell every man, woman, and child on this planet today what they should do and think and feel. He has absolute and total authority over your life and over cities and states and nations. The risen Christ is great — greater than you have ever imagined.

> Here is our witness to the world: The risen Christ is your king and has absolute, unlimited authority over your life. If you do not bow and worship him and trust him and obey him, you commit high treason against Christ the King, who is God over all. The resurrection is God's open declaration that he lays claim on every person and tribe and tongue and nation…'All authority on earth is mine.' Your sex life is his to rule; your business is his to rule; your career is his to rule; your home is his; your children are his, your vacation is his, your body is his; He is *God*! So if you resist his claim, feel no admiration for his infinite power and authority, and turn finally to seek satisfaction from thrills that allow you to be your own master, then you will be executed for treason in the last day. And it will appear so reasonable and so right that you should be executed for your disloyalty to your Maker and Redeemer that there will be no appeals and no objections. Your life of

indifference to the risen Christ and of half-hearted attention now and then to a few of his commandments will appear on that day as supremely blameworthy and infinitely foolish, and you will...weep that you did not change" ("Worship the Risen Christ", 4-3-83).

Obey His Authoritative Plan
Matthew 28:19-20

Commenting on Matthew 28:19, John Calvin wrote, "Now the wall is pulled down and the Lord orders the ministers of the gospel to go far out to scatter the teaching of salvation throughout all the regions of the earth" (George, 39). Tragically many in Carey's day, as well as our own, have imbibed the spirit of the 18th century anti-missions hymn: *Go into all the world, the Lord of old did say. But now where He has planted thee, there thou shouldst stay.*

Carey would have no part of this spiritually bankrupt and impotent thinking. Rather, having his heart gripped by the words of our Savior, he said, "I care not where or how I lived, or what hardships I went through, so that I could but gain souls for Christ. While I was asleep I dreamed of these things, and when I awoke the first thing I thought of was this great work. All my desire was for the conversion of the heathen, and all my hope was in God" (George 45).

The imperative or command of verse 19 is "make disciples." The "therefore" links the command to the "all authority" declaration of verse 18. Further, wed to an imperative, the three participles - going, baptizing and teaching - orbiting in the same galaxy, receive the force and thrust of imperatives. Thus Jesus charges us, commands us to make disciples by going, make disciples by baptizing, and make disciples by teaching.

Make Disciples by Going, Matthew 28:19

There is no need to pray and ask God if we should go and take the gospel to the nations. We have been told to go. Again, John Piper says:

> So there you have the word of God from the mouth of Jesus. The lofty claim: 'All authority is given to me.' The loving comfort: 'I am with you always, even to the end of the age.' The last command: 'Go make disciples among all the peoples of the world.' What is clear from this final word of Jesus is that he is trying to move us to act. He not only says, 'Go make disciples.' He also gives us a warrant for doing it so that we can know it is a legitimate and right thing to do: All authority in heaven and on earth is his. He gives us tremendous encouragement and comfort and strength to go, with the promise that he would go with us and never leave us. Jesus ended his earthly life with these words because he wanted us to respond. He was motivating us to act (*The Lofty Claim, the Last Command, the Loving Comfort*, 11-1-98).

Do you need a reason to go? No! You need a reason to stay! 1.6 billion people have yet to hear the name of Jesus.

R.T. France captures the theological thrust of Jesus' command to go when he says, "Jesus' vision of the future heavenly enthronement of the Son of Man in Matthew 24:30 led naturally into a mission to gather his chosen people from all over the earth (24:31)...But the agents of this ingathering are not now to be angels... but those who are already Jesus' disciples" (*Matthew*, NICNT, 1114).

Go and make more followers, more disciples of Jesus. Go, and where? All the nations.

In his journal entry on March 29, 1794, Carey wrote, "O what is there in all this world worth living for but the presence and service of God – I feel a burning desire that all the world may know this God and serve Him."

Go and make disciples.

Make Disciples by Baptizing, Matthew 28:19

Here is the badge of being a disciple. Here is where biblical profession of faith takes place. Here is my unashamed identification with Jesus as my Lord by public declaration.

Baptism – immersion, plain and clear.

Name – singular.

Father, Son and Holy Spirit – Father, Savior, and Comforter, the Triune God.

What joy to initiate new believers into the church of the Lord Jesus as they identify themselves with Christ in death, burial and resurrection. And that they would be found in every nation and from all the peoples of the earth! What a gospel! What a mission! What an assignment!

Closing his *Enquiry* with a word of missionary encouragement Carey wrote, "What a heaven will it be to see the many myriads of poor heathens... who by their labors have been brought to the knowledge of God. Surely a "crown of rejoicing" (1 Thessalonians 2:19) like this is worth aspiring to. Surely it is worth while to lay ourselves out with all our might in promoting the cause and kingdom of Christ" (57).

Make Disciples by Teaching, Matthew 28:20

We do not make converts. We are called to make disciples, "little Christs", who observe all His teachings. James Boice well says, "Robust disciples are not made by watered-down teaching" (*Gospel of Matthew*, 649). A "hit & run" approach to missions and ministry will fail to accomplish this. Short-term endeavors, though commendable and valuable, are no substitute for those who give years, even the rest of their lives, to teach others who can teach others who can teach others.

Baptism is preschool enrollment into a school of learning that one never graduates from! But someone must go and teach them.

Trust His Amazing Promise
Matthew 28:20

William Carey was a great man, but he was a man. Life brought him many tragedies. Francis Wayland said of him, "Like most of the master minds of all ages, Carey was educated in the school of adversity" (George, 94). There were times when his soul was plunged to the depths of depression. He would bury 2 wives, with his first, Dorothy, sorrowfully, going insane. He would bury three children, and certain others disappointed him. He lost most of his hair due to illness in his early 20s, served in India for 41 years never taking a furlough, fought back dysentery and malaria, and did not baptize his first Indian convert, Krisha Pal, until his seventh year on the field! What kept him going? What promise of God did He claim again and again in the face of discouragement and defeat? He had asked his friend John Williams in 1801, "Pray for us that we may be faithful to the end" (George,

154). He was! How? This promise: "And lo, I am with you always, even to the end of the age."

Two aspects to this amazing promise sustained Carey, and they will sustain us as well wherever the Lord might send us.

He will be with you constantly ("always"). He will be with you continually ("to the end of the age"). Knowing God was with him constantly and continually saw Carey through those valleys of the shadow of death, "dungeons of despair," and feelings of total inadequacy.

In a letter to his father he wrote concerning his call:

> I see more and more of my own insufficiency for the great work I am called to. The truths of God are amazingly profound, the souls of men infinitely precious, my own ignorance very great and all that I do is for God who knows my motives and my ends, my diligence or negligence. When I (in short) compare myself with my work, I sink into a point, a mere despicable nothing. (George, 25).

In his journal entry dated Aug. 27-31, 1794, Carey wrote:

> **August 27**
> Nothing new, my Soul is in general barren and unfruitful; Yet I find a pleasure in drawing near to God; and a peculiar sweetness in His Holy Word. I find it more & more to be a very precious treasure.

> **August 28-30**
> Nothing of any importance except to my shame, a prevalence of carnality, negligence, and spiritual deadness; no heart for private duties, indeed everything seems to be going to

decay in my soul, and I almost despair of being any use to the heathen at all.

August 31

Was somewhat engaged more than of late in the things of God, felt some new devotedness to God, and desired to live entirely to him, and for his glory; O that I could live always as under his eye, and feel a sense of his immediate presence, this is life and all besides this is death to my soul.

G. Campbell Morgan was reading Matthew 28:20 to an 85-year-old saint. Finishing the verse he said, "That is a great promise. She looked up and said sharply, with the light of sanctified humor in her eyes; "That is not a promise at all, that is a fact. Oh, if the church of God could remember that fact!"

Conclusion

Matthew 28 begins with a resurrection and ends with a commission. These final words of our Lord are weighty, heavy, and not easily digested. They do not need an adrenalin response. They need a cardiac response, a heart response. They need a response that has carefully considered the King who speaks them, and the kind of servant who obeys them. Once more hear the words of William Carey, who heard and heeded His Master's call.

A Christian minister is a person who is "not his own" (1Cor. 6:19); he is the servant of God, and therefore ought to be wholly devoted to him. By entering on that sacred office he solemnly undertakes to be always engaged as much as possible in the Lord's work, and not to choose his own pleasure or employment, or pursue the ministry as something that is to subserve his own ends or interest, or as a kind of sideline. He engages to go where God pleases, and to do or endure what he sees fit to command or call him to in the exercise of his function. He virtually bids farewell to friends, pleasures, and comforts, and stands in readiness to endure the greatest sufferings in the work of the Lord, his Master. It is inconsistent for ministers to please themselves with thoughts of numerous congregations, cordial friends, a civilized country, legal protection, affluence, splendor, or even an income that is sufficient. The slights and hatred of men, and even pretended friends, gloomy prisons, and tortures, the society of barbarians of uncouth speech, miserable accommodations in wretched wildernesses, hunger and thirst, nakedness, weariness, and diligence, hard work, and but little worldly encouragement, should rather be the objects of their expectation.... I question whether all are justified in staying here, while so many are perishing without means of grace in other lands.... On the contrary the commission is a sufficient call to them to venture all, and, like the primitive Christians, go everywhere preaching the gospel. (50).

On his 70th birthday, 3 years before his death, Carey would give his own humble evaluation of his life and ministry. Herein we discover something of the man that made him great for God. In a letter to his son Jabez he wrote:

I am this day seventy years old, a monument of Divine mercy and goodness, though on a review of my life I find much, very much, for which I ought to be humbled in the dust; my direct and positive sins are innumerable, my negligence in the Lord's

work has been great, I have not promoted his cause, nor sought his glory and honor as I ought, notwithstanding all this, I am spared till now, and am still retained in his Work, and I trust I am receive into the divine favor through him. I wish to be more entirely dovoted to his service, more completely sanctified and more habitually exercising all the Christian graces, and bringing forth the fruits of righteousness to the praise and honor of that Savior who gave his life a sacrifice for sin. (George, 155).

After he died on June 9, 1834, these simple words would be inscribed on the stone slab that marked his grave in Serampore, India: "A wretched, poor, and helpless worm, on thy kind arms I fall" (George, 168). Would to God that He would raise up from among us an army of such wretched, poor and helpless worms. The world needs them. Jesus deserves them. Our churches should provide them.

*Citations from Carey's journal are from *The Journal and Selected Letters of Williams Carey*, edited by Terry G. Carter.

Marked for Death, Messengers of Life: Adoniram & Ann Judson

꙰

Romans 8: 28-39

Adoniram Judson is the father of the American Baptist missionary movement. Eugene Harrison calls him "the apostle of the love of Christ in Burma." He left American soil as a Congregationalist. Arriving in India, having carefully studied the New Testament, he became a Baptist. He was baptized by an associate of William Carey. He would eventually go to Burma where he labored for nearly 40 years. He would translate the whole Bible into Burmese, spend 21 months in a brutal prison, and bury 2 wives and more than five children. Divine providence indeed marked him for death, while also making him a messenger of life.

Born in 1788 in Massachusetts, he would die in 1850 and be buried at sea. No earthly grave marks his departure from this world into the world of his King Jesus. Fred Barlow said it well when he wrote, "by whatever measurement you measure the man Judson, the measurement always is the same — he was a mighty man!"

Romans 8:28-39 is written "all over the life" of this wonderful Baptist missionary. Indeed, had he not been confident of the truths contained in these verses, he would have never "finished the race" and "kept the faith" (2 Tim. 4:8). Many of us will likewise be sustained only by the same.

Four lessons leap from this text for our blessing and benefit. Each was marvelously lived out by Adoniram and Ann Judson. Each comes in the form of a divine promise.

We Have His Providence
Romans 8:28-32

Paul affirms that there are no accidents in the life of the child of God, only providence. In 8:28 we are given a: certain promise (we know); comprehensive promise (all things); comforting promise (work together for good); chosen promise (those who love God); clear promise (called according to His purpose). Paul also affirms the signed, sealed and settled nature of our salvation through what has been called the "golden chain of redemption."

The chain has five links, located in verses 29-30. First, God foreknew. Second, He predestined. Third, He called. Fourth, He justified. Fifth, He glorified. These are certain realities in the plan and purpose of God. Such a glorious and certain salvation has very definite and wonderful consequences: God is for us (v. 31) and He will give us everything we need for His glory and our good (v. 32).

How did this divine providence work itself out in Judson's life? Let me note three ways.

First, his family and education. Mentally – he was a giant. He began reading at the age of three, took navigation lessons at ten, studied theology as a child, and entered Providence College (now Brown University) at seventeen. Despite the fact that his father was a Congregational preacher, and in spite of his mother's "tears and pleadings," Judson was not saved until he was 20 years of age. In college he became a confirmed deist – due largely to the influence of a brilliant unbelieving student at Brown who set out to win Judson to his deistic faith. That man was Jacob Eames of Belfast, Maine. Keep that name in mind.

Second, his conversion. No conversion, save the apostle Paul's, is any more providential in its character than that of Adoniram. After graduation he left home to become a wanderlust (a traveler in search of excitement), confirmed and growing in his deistic convictions. One night, while traveling, he stopped to stay in a country inn. His room was adjacent to the room of a dying man. The moaning and groaning of that man through the long night permitted Judson no sleep. His thoughts troubled him. All night questions assailed his soul: "Was the dying man prepared to die? Where would he spend eternity? Was he a Christian, calm and strong in the hope of life in Heaven? Or, was he a sinner shuddering in the dark brink of the lower region?" Judson constantly chided himself for even entertaining such thoughts contrary to his philosophy of life beyond the grave, and thought how his brilliant college friend would rebuke him if he learned of these childish worries.

But the next morning, when Judson was leaving, he was informed that the man had died. He inquired of the proprietor as to the identity of the dead man. He was shocked by the staggering statement that he heard: "He was a brilliant young person from Providence College. Eames was his name" (Anderson, 44).

Jacob Eames was the unbeliever who had destroyed Judson's faith. "Now he was dead—and was lost! Was lost! Was lost! Lost! Lost!" Those words raced through his brain, rang in his ears, roared in his soul — "Was lost! Lost! Lost!" There and then Judson realized he was lost, too! He immediately ended his traveling, returned home, and entered Andover Theological Seminary. Soon he "sought God for the saving of his soul." Shortly thereafter he was saved and he dedicated his life to the Master's service!

Joining a group at Andover called "the Brethren," an outgrowth of the famous "Haystack Revival," he would answer God's call to be a missionary. This would lead him to turn down golden opportunities both at Brown and an influential church in Plymouth. The latter broke the heart of his mother who on hearing of the offer rejoiced and said, "And you will be so near home."

Judson, however, replied, "I shall never live in Boston. I have further than that to go." Neither the tears of his mother and sister nor the hopes and dreams of his father could deter him from his call to go to the nations for Jesus' sake.

Third, his wife. God led Judson both to the right woman and, I should add, the right father-in-law. Ann (Nancy) Hasseltine would become the first woman missionary from America to go overseas. She would die at the young age of 37. The 2 children she bore (she also miscarried at least once) would die in infancy, Roger Williams at 8 months and Maria at 27 months.

Ann was saved at 16 and married Adoniram when she was 23. Brilliant in her own right, she learned Burmese and Siamese, did translation work, and cared for her husband tirelessly during his imprisonment. There is little doubt this dedication cost her her life.

Having been smitten by Ann, Adoniram wrote a letter to her father asking for her hand in marriage, and also one to Ann where he lays bare his heart for her and the mission with which God had burdened his soul. Both letters are legendary among missionaries.

The letter to Mr. Hasseltine:

> I have now to ask whether you can consent to part with your daughter early next spring, to see her no more in this world? Whether you can consent to her departure to a heathen land, and her subjection to the hardships and sufferings of a missionary life? Whether you can consent to her exposure to the dangers of the ocean; to the fatal influence of the southern climate of India; to every kind of want and distress; to degradation, insult, persecution, and perhaps a violent death? Can you consent to all this, for the sake of Him who left His heavenly home and died for her and for you; for the sake of perishing, immortal souls; for the sake of Zion and the glory of God? Can you consent to all this, in hope of soon meeting your daughter in the world of glory, with a crown of righteousness brightened by the acclamations of praise which shall redound to her Savior from heathens saved, through her means, from eternal woe and despair?

The letter to Ann (Jan. 1, 1811):

> It is with the utmost sincerity, and with my whole heart, that I wish you, my love, a happy new year. May it be a year in which your walk will be close with God; your frame calm and serene; and the road that leads you to the Lamb marked with purer

light. May it be a year in which you will have more largely the spirit of Christ, be raised above sublunary things, and be willing to be disposed of in this world just as God shall please. As every moment of the year will bring you nearer the end of your pilgrimage, may it bring you nearer to God, and find you more prepared to hail the messenger of death as a deliverer and a friend. And now, since I have begun to wish, I will go on. May this be the year in which you will change your name; in which you will take a final leave of your relatives and native land; in which you will cross the wide ocean, and dwell on the other side of the world, among a heathen people. What a great change will this year probably effect in our lives! How very different will be our situation and employment! If our lives are preserved and our attempt prospered, we shall next new year's day be in India, and perhaps wish each other a happy new year in the uncouth dialect of Hindostan or Burmah. We shall no more see our kind friends around us, or enjoy the conveniences of civilized life, or go to the house of God with those that keep holy day; but swarthy countenances will everywhere meet our eye, the jargon of an unknown tongue will assail our ears, and we shall witness the assembling of the heathen to celebrate the worship of idol gods. We shall be weary of the world, and wish for wings like a dove, that we may fly away and be at rest. We shall probably experience seasons when we shall be 'exceeding sorrowful, even unto death.' We shall see many dreary, disconsolate hours, and feel a sinking of spirits, anguish of mind, of which now we can form little conception. O, we shall wish to lie down and die. And that time may soon come. One of us may be unable to sustain the heat of the climate and the change of habits; and the other

may say, with literal truth, over the grave -
  'By foreign hands thy dying eyes were closed;
  By foreign hands thy decent limbs composed;
  By foreign hands thy humble grave adorned.'
But whether we shall be honored and mourned by strangers, God only knows. At least, either of us will be certain of one mourner. In view of such scenes shall we not pray with earnestness 'O for an overcoming faith?'

Thirteen months later they would marry. A few days after that they sailed for Calcutta on their way, by unseen providence, to Rangoon, Burma. Yes, the child of God has the Lord's providence.

We Have His Prayers
Romans 8:33-34

The child of God has a double divine blessing in the department of prayer. In vs. 26-27 we learn that the Spirit of God prays in us. In vs. 33-34 we learn that in heaven the Son of God prays for us. In heart and in heaven deity intercedes for the child of God.

In v. 33 the theme of our justification is brought forward once again (cf. v. 30). Using a courtroom analogy, Paul points out no one can successfully bring a charge or accusation that will stick against a believer because God has declared us just from His bar as judge.

Verse 34 builds on v. 33 and settles the issue decisively once and for all. Who can charge or condemn us at the judgment with the hope that we will be found guilty? Again the answer is no one! Why? Four reasons are given. First, Christ died [for us]. Second, He is raised [for us]. Third, He is exalted at God's right hand [for us]. Fourth, He continually makes intercession for us (cf. Heb. 7:25).

Hallelujah! What a Savior!

Knowing of the intercession of Jesus was crucial to Judson. Sometimes it was all he had to lean on in the midst of sorrow and suffering. How so?

Arriving in India, the East India Company forced the Judsons to leave as they tried to settle at different places. They lived four months on the Isle of France, where they learned of the death of Mrs. Harriett Newell, Ann's best friend, a 19-year-old teen who had sailed with them from America to serve as a fellow missionary. Harriett died while giving birth to her baby girl on the cabin floor of a ship with only her husband at her side. The baby also died, and so would her husband soon thereafter. The Judsons finally found a resting place on July 13, 1812, at Rangoon, Burma. Here, by their sweat, labor and blood the gospel would be planted among the hostile Burmese peoples.

In Rangoon the first ten years of missionary labors were given mainly to the mastering of the Burmese language. They had no grammar, dictionary or English-speaking teacher. Three years after their arrival, Adoniram completed a grammar for the Burmese language. On May 20, 1817, he finished the translation of Matthew; he also wrote tracts — concise, clear statements of Bible truth — and gave them out discriminately and prayerfully.

After almost seven years in Burma, on April 4, 1819, Adoniram ventured to preach his first public discourse. Sitting in a traditional Burmese zayat by the roadside he would call out, "Ho! Everyone that thirsteth for knowledge." (TGS, 221). On June 27 he baptized Moung Hau, his first Burmese convert. Soon others who had also been taught would follow. By 1822 there were 18 converts he could count after 10 years of laboring.

In 1824 war broke out between Burma and the English government of India and the Judsons were looked upon as English spies. On June 8, 1824, Judson was arrested and put first in what many called "the Death Prison," the horrible prison of Oung-pen-la. The dimensions of "the Death Prison" were forty by thirty feet, five feet high, with no ventilation other than the cracks between the boards.

In this room were confined one hundred persons of both sexes and all nationalities, nearly all naked, and half famished. The prison was never washed or even swept. Putrid remains of animal and vegetable matter, together with nameless abominations, strewed the floor. In this place of torment Mr. Judson lay with five pairs of fetters on his legs and ankles, weighing about fourteen pounds, the marks of which he carried to his dying day. At nightfall, lest the prisoners should escape, a bamboo pole was placed between the legs and then drawn up by means of pulleys to a height which allowed only their shoulders to rest on the ground while their feet depended from the iron rings of the fetters.

Mosquitoes would often land and eat away the broken flesh of their feet, nearly driving them mad. Adoniram endured 21 months of prison life, nearly dying on several occasions. Of the British POWs, all but one would die.

Judson was not the only sufferer. His wife Ann was without support or protection. Yet she brought food to the prison day after day, and with bribes passed the officials and gave relief to her husband and some of the other suffering prisoners. She gave birth to a child, and after 21 days carried the little girl in her arms to show to her father in prison. The child contracted smallpox; then the mother herself was

Five Who Changed The World

inflicted with the same disease, followed closely by spotted fever, which brought her close to death. After many petitions, she secured permission for her husband to come out of prison, and he, with fetters on and a guard following, carried their crying baby about the streets, begging Burman mothers to nurse the child. Ann could not nurse her own little girl, she was so emaciated and weak.

During this time Adoniram and Ann tried to remain strong, despite the fact that their health deteriorated and death nearly claimed each of them on numerous occasions. Judson once remarked, "it is possible my life will be spared, if so, with what zeal shall I pursue my work! If not — His will be done. The door will be open for others who will do the work better." (TGS, 334).

Later, toward the end of his imprisonment, his faith would be severely tested. Courtney Anderson summarizes the situation: "His daughter was starving before his eyes; Ann was nearly dead, his translation was lost; he himself was marked for death" (TGS, 349).

I am convinced it was the prayers of the Savior that sustained him during those days.

We Have His Power
Romans 8:35-37

Life, by its very nature, is filled with sorrow and suffering, hardships and disappointments. Yet, no thing in this life can conquer the child of God. Why? We have His prayers (v. 34) and His love (vs. 37 and 39) which gives us the victory.

In v. 35 Paul notes the realities that will come against but cannot conquer the child of God. In v. 36 he passionately notes the precious lives given for the sake of King Jesus. This destiny was foretold in Ps.

44:22.

Yet in all of this and more, we are "more than conquerors," *hupernikomen;* "super conquerors" through Him who loves us. Do you see it? His great power is wedded to and made active by His great love, a power that can keep us going "against all odds!"

Adoniram Judson desperately needed to know this. Eventually he was released from prison. He quickly made his way to Ann and little Maria. Read what he met in the words of Eugene Harrison:

> One of the most pathetic pages in the history of Christian missions is that which describes the scene when Judson was finally released and returned to the mission house seeking Ann, who again had failed to visit him for some weeks. As he ambles down the street as fast as his maimed ankles would permit, the tormenting question kept repeating itself, "is Ann still alive?" Upon reaching the house, the first object to attract his attention was a fat, half-naked Burman woman squatting in the ashes beside a pan of coals and holding on her knees an emaciated baby, so begrimed with dirt that it did not occur to him that it could be his own. Across the foot of the bed, as though she had fallen there, lay a human object that, at the first glance, was no more recognizable than his child. The face was of a ghastly paleness and the body shrunken to the last degree of emaciation. The glossy black curls had all been shorn from the finely-shaped head. There lay the faithful and devoted wife who had followed him so unwearily from prison to prison, ever alleviating his distresses and consoling him in his trials. Presently Ann felt warm tears falling upon her face and, rousing from her daze, saw Adoniram at her side. She suffered from spotted fever and cerebral meningitis.

Amazingly she survived, but only briefly. In less than a year, while away out of necessity, he received what is known as "the blacked sealed letter." Told by its deliverer that he was sorry to inform Adoniram of the death of his little Maria, he opened the letter only to read: "My Dear Sir: To one who has suffered so much and with such exemplary fortitude, there needs but little preface to tell a tale of distress. It was cruel indeed to torture you with doubt and suspense. To sum up the unhappy tidings in a few words – Mrs. Judson is no more. (TGS, 370).

Ann had died a month earlier while he was away. His beautiful and faithful helper had gone to be with her King. Six months later, on April 24, 1827, little Maria slipped into eternity and into the arms of Jesus, united so quickly to her mother.

Death seemed to be all about Adoniram. For a period of months he was plunged into despair and depression. He would flee to the jungle and live the life of a hermit, for some time questioning himself, his calling, even his faith. He demanded all his letters to America be destroyed (TGS, 390). He renounced the D.D. degree bestowed upon him by Brown.

He gave all his private wealth, a sizable sum, to the Baptist Mission Board. He requested a cut in salary.

He dug a grave near his Hermitage and for days sat beside it staring into it. On October 24, 1829, the third anniversary of Ann's death, he would write, "God is to me the Great Unknown. I believe in Him, but I find Him not" (TGS, 391). However, God's power and love did not fail him. He would emerge from the valley of the shadow of death in the strength of his Good Shepherd. He would say of these days, "there is a love that never fails. If I had not felt certain that every additional trial was ordered by infinite love and mercy, I could not have survived my accumulated sufferings."

Adoniram Judson would marry twice more. In 1834 he married Sarah Boardman, a precious and wonderful lady who had lost her missionary husband in death. They were married for 11 years, and she would bear him eight children, five of whom would survive into adulthood. In 1846 he married Emily Chabbuck. They would spend not quite four years together as Adoniram died on April 12, 1850. Emily died four years later in New York of tuberculosis, another slaughtered sheep for her Savior.

We Have His Promise
Romans 8: 38-39

These final verses of Romans 8 constitute what some call "the grand persuasion." Added to the seven items of verse 35 are nine additional realities that have no hope, no chance, of separating the child of God from the love of God found in Christ Jesus our Lord.

Such a promise accompanied Adoniram, who would finish his Burmese translation of the Bible on January 31, 1834. He did a complete revision that was finished in 1840.

Adoniram would live to see about 7,000 people baptized in Burma by the time of his death, and 63 congregations were established under 163 missionaries, native pastors and assistants. Today the Myanmar Baptist Convention has more than 600,000 members in 3,513 churches. All of this goes back to the work of God accomplished through the Judsons.

Then there is the matter of the Karen people and the movement of God among them. This in and of itself is a remarkable evidence of the providence of God preparing a particular people for the gospel. Here is the historical record of what occurred.

In the year 1828 an event of vast significance took place. Having come in contact with the Karens, a race of wild people living in remote and almost inaccessible jungles, Judson longed for the opportunity of winning a Karen for Christ and thus reaching his race. This opportunity came to him through Ko Tha Byu, a Karen slave who was sold one day in the bazaar in Moulmein and bought by a native Christian, who forthwith brought him to Judson to be taught and, if possible, evangelized. Ko Tha Byu was a desperate robber bandit. He had taken part in approximately thirty murders and was a hardened criminal with a vicious nature and an ungovernable temper. Patiently, prayerfully, and lovingly, Judson instructed the wretched, depraved creature, who eventually not only yielded to the transforming power of Christ but went through the jungles as a flaming evangelist among his people. The hearts of the Karens had been remarkably and providentially prepared for the reception of the gospel message by a tradition prevalent among them to this effect:

Long, long ago the Karen elder brother and his young white brother lived close together. God gave each of them a Book of Gold containing all they needed for their salvation, success and happiness. The Karen brother neglected and lost his Book of Gold and so he fell into a wretched type of existence, ignorant and cruelly oppressed by the Burmese. The white brother, however, prized his Golden Book, or Book of God, and so, when he sailed away across the oceans, God greatly blessed him. Some day the white brother will return, bringing with him God's Book, which, if the Karen people will receive and obey, will bring to them salvation and untold blessings.

Accordingly, as Ko Tha Byu went on his unwearying preaching tours through the jungles, declaring that the long-looked-for white brother had returned with God's Book, hundreds received the message with gladness.

When a depraved slave, a bandit and murderer, was brought to Judson in 1828, who would have imagined that, a century later, the Christian Karens would have many splendid high schools, hundreds of village schools, some 800 self-supporting churches and a Christian constituency of more than 150,000?

Conclusion

On March 4, 1831, Adoniram Judson wrote a letter to his fellow missionary Cephas Bennett, who was a printer, requesting 15,000 to 20,000 tracks. Attending the great annual Buddist festival at the Shwe Dagon in Rangoon, they experienced a mighty movement of God's Spirit and an increased interest in the gospel. May his words burn deep into our hearts, never to depart:

[We have distributed] nearly ten thousand tracts, giving to none but those who ask. I presume there have been six thousand applications at the house. Some come two or three months' journey, from the borders of Siam and China — 'Sir, we hear that there is an eternal hell. We are afraid of it. Do give us a writing that will tell us how to escape it.' Others come from the frontiers of Kathay, a hundred miles north of Ava — 'Sir, we have seen a writing that tells about an eternal God. Are you the man that gives away such writings? If so, pray give us one, for we want to know the truth before we die.' Others come from the interior of the country, where the name of

33

Jesus Christ is a little known — 'Are you Jesus Christ's man? Give us a writing that tells about Jesus Christ.' (TGS, 399).

*Significant biographical information on Judson came from *To the Golden Shore* by Courtney Anderson.

.

Jesus is Everything to Me!: Glorious Truth in the Life and Death of Bill Wallace

Philippians 1:21

William Wallace emerged from relative obscurity to become a national hero. A man of great courage and giftedness, he was tragically cut down in the prime of his life. His people mourned his death. Dedicated to what he believed in, he knowingly and willingly shunned a safer game plan and course of action that would have certainly extended his natural life. Arrested and brutally tortured, beaten and ridiculed, he would die alone with no words of comfort and no one to console him. Much like the apostle Paul in the cold, damp Mamertine dungeon in Rome, he died with no one at his side (2 Tim. 4).

Now, you might find it odd and even out of place that I would dare to draw a comparison between William Wallace of Scotland and the Apostle Paul. But then I suspect you probably have the wrong William Wallace in mind, for I am not interested in that William Wallace (of

Braveheart fame), but William (Bill) Wallace the missionary, a man who served the Chinese people for 15 years only to be brutally murdered as a martyr on February 10, 1951.

When I think of "Bill Wallace of China" as he is affectionately known, Philippians 1:21 immediately comes to my mind. This is my life verse. Anytime I have the honor of putting my signature in a copy of the Bible, I will append this verse. It is my prayer for my life, my heart's desire in my service for the Lord Jesus. As Paul says in the verse immediately preceding this text, my goal in life is that "Christ will be magnified in my body, whether by life or by death" (Phil. 1:20). Bill Wallace of China did both.

For Me To Live Is Christ

Bill Wallace was a Jesus-intoxicated man. For Bill to live was Christ. He proclaimed the gospel of Jesus Christ by word and deed, quietly and without much fanfare to be sure, but effectively without question.

Bill Wallace was born in 1908 in Tennessee, the son of a physician. Initially he had little interest in medicine, but loved things mechanical including cars and motorcycles. This was providential as it prepared him for a number of unique challenges on the mission field.

At the age of 17, while working on a car in the family garage, a nagging question haunted him once again: "What should I do with my life? No, what would God have me do with my life?" Simply, quietly, with a New Testament in his hand, the decisive decision was made: he would be a medical missionary. The date was July 5, 1925. He never looked back or wavered from this commitment.

Wallace would spend the next 10 years receiving his education to become a doctor. He would turn down a lucrative offer of a medical practice in the states.

As the time of his medical training drew to a close, a prayer was going up in the ancient China city of Wuchow. Dr. Robert Beddoe needed help at the Stout Memorial Hospital. Writing to the Foreign Mission Board he pled, "O God, give us a surgeon." At almost the same time Bill Wallace was penning his own letter to the Foreign Mission Board. Here is what he wrote.

> **My name is William L. Wallace and I am now serving as a resident in surgery at Knoxville General Hospital, Knoxville, Tennessee. Since my senior year in high school, I have felt God would have me to be a medical missionary, and to that end I have been preparing myself. I attended the University of Tennessee for my premedical work and received the M.D. from the University Medical School in Memphis. I did an internship here at Knoxville General and remained for a surgical residency.**
>
> **I am not sure what you desire by way of information, but I am single, twenty-six years old, and I am a member of the Broadway Baptist Church. My mother died when I was eleven and my father, also a physician, passed away two years ago. There were only two of us, and my sister, Ruth Lynn, is planning marriage.**
>
> **I must confess, I am not a good speaker nor apt as a teacher, but I do feel God can use my training as a physician. As humbly as I know how, I want to volunteer to serve as a medical missionary under our Southern Baptist Foreign Mission Board. I have always thought of Africa, but I will go**

anywhere I am needed.

On July 25, 1935, ten years to the month from the time he made his garage commitment and recorded it on the back leaf of his New Testament, Bill was appointed as a medical missionary to Wuchow, South China.

For Bill Wallace, Jesus Christ was everything. Read what this quiet, shy man said to his home church, Broadway Baptist, on September 1, 1935, five weeks after his appointment and just prior to his leaving for China:

> I want to express to you my sincere and heartfelt appreciation in making it possible for me to go to China as your missionary, your ambassador for the Lord Jesus Christ ... You may ask why do I want to go to China ... and there spend my life and energy. You might say there is much to be done in this country and many have said you can do a lot of good here. Why should I go when there are such hardships and inconveniences? The only answer I have is that it is God's plan that I go.
>
> And God's call was so definite to me. I think he made it definite for me so that there would be no doubt in my mind as to God's plan. So that through the long years of preparation there would be no doubt that I was doing God's will. That has been a comfort and joy to me and I have often thought, "If God can be for me who can be against me."
>
> I want to go because of the needs. And how great is that need! China today is ready and willing to hear and accept the gospel of the Lord Jesus. In Luke 10:2 we read, "the harvest truly is great, ... pray ye therefore ... that he would send forth laborers into the harvest." In our mission field today in China and in

other countries, hundreds and thousands are going to their death without knowledge of the Lord Jesus Christ because we do not have enough missionaries to tell the story.

I want to go to China because someone has prayed ... and God heard these prayers and has answered as he always does when God's people pray. I would rather be going out as God's missionary this morning than anything else in the world.

If there is one final word or request that I leave with you it is this— that you would pray for me, pray daily that this, your humble servant's ministry and work might be all that God would have it to be.

Bill Wallace was all about Jesus. This would affect a number of important decisions in his life. For example, Bill Wallace would never marry. In 1935 there was a young lady he took with him to Ridgecrest, N.C. Many expected them to marry. However, the young lady later said, "[Marriage] was out of the question. It would have been bigamy; Bill Wallace was already married to his work!"

To Die Is Gain

China was a boiling cauldron of political instability before Bill Wallace even arrived. However he was undeterred. Upon his initial arrival in Wuchow, he was informed that he would immediately have to return to Hong Kong because of the unrest. Bill simply and firmly said no. Informed that the captain was upset by his answer and could not be responsible for his safety Bill laughed and said, "Tell your captain to rest easy. He was not responsible for my coming here in the first place, and he doesn't need to be responsible for my staying here!"

Bill would love and serve the Chinese people for 15 years. His commitment kept him in China through a number of political uprisings, the Japanese invasion of China, World War II, and the Communist takeover of China. On more than a few occasions he would perform surgery with bombs exploding all around the hospital. Dr. Wallace sent this following letter to his sister; Ruth Wallace Stegall, on September 17, 1938.

> **Dear Sister:**
>
> **Our hospital, our school, and houses were bombed yesterday at 11 a.m. One bomb hit right in middle of hospital and 3 on the side. We are all safe. None of the hospital employees killed. A few hurt. Hospital is full of wounded.**
>
> **Don't worry. We are all safe. Don't have time to write more.**
>
> **Don't worry.**
>
> **William**

At one point, he was forced to abandon Wuchow but kept the hospital going as he helped move it by boat up the river. This is where his mechanical expertise was especially helpful! Again and again he was urged to leave China but his response was steadfast, "I will stay as long as I am able to serve." And serve he did

Once a small child died in his hospital. The parents came. Heartbroken and grieving, he loved and ministered to them. He sat down with them and told them of Jesus and His love for the little children including their own. (Fletcher, 53).

During his tenure Dr. Beddoe spoke of a revival that broke out in the hospital since Dr. Wallace's arrival. People were, he said, being healed and saved in Stout Memorial Hospital. He dated the beginning of the Spirit's movement with the arrival of Bill.

Read the testimony of his love and ministry to the Chinese people:

> It was while at Fok-Luk that I saw Dr. Wallace refuse his rice allowance and give it to a nurse who was desperately ill with fever. Most of us were sick with diarrhea or fever. Later on I saw him behind the cook tent we had rigged up. He was eating grains of burned rice, hardly palatable, that had been thrown away. When he realized I had seen him, he was terribly embarrassed.
>
> No, he wasn't ashamed of eating that food. No one else would have had it, as hungry as we were. I think he was embarrassed because he did not want me to know how hungry he was.
>
> He was so thin I thought he would blow away if a good wind came along. Somehow, however, he stayed well. He showed us how to eat the bones of what few fowl we found, to get needed vitamins. I believe his unorthodox methods saved all our lives during this period. He was so good, watching over each of us, cheering us, caring for the sick, and doing everything he could to provide for our comfort.
>
> I don't want to offend you, Miss Wright, but we Chinese are not used to seeing Americans or Europeans do things like this. We know the missionaries love us, but there was always a difference. They lived their way and we lived ours, but Dr. Wallace didn't know about the difference. He was one of us. He accepted our portion — all of it." (137-138).

What was said about Bill Wallace?

"If you want to find him, find the sickest patient in the hospital, and there he will be." (95).

Bill Wallace was a doctor. His basic ministry was one of healing. But he was in China first of all as a bearer of the good news of Jesus Christ, the glad tidings of forgiveness and eternal life inherent in the old, old message of God's love. Sometimes his soft, stuttering witness to that grace was more effective than the most eloquent evangelist's plea (89).

"With me, it's different. I'm the one to stay. I'm just one piece of man without other responsibilities" (Bill Wallace).

One piece of man—it was an old Chinese saying used courteously to depreciate one's value. It indicated a single, unencumbered, expendable person. By it, Bill meant his life was the only one at stake. He was the one thus seated by circumstances, prepared by God for this moment. He was the one to stay on in the face of the unknown, to give the Stout Memorial Hospital and the Baptist witness every chance to continue living, once the Red blight arrived.

'I'm just one piece of man...,' Ed Galloway repeated the conversation to his wife as the ferry carried them to Hong Kong. 'He really meant it. He has no concept of his own worth and no anxiety for the future that I can see.' (177).

By a Chinese believer concerning their beloved "Waa I Saang", as they called him: "He actually lived before us the life of Christ."

What was said by Bill Wallace?

" I am more aware of my limitations than I have ever been. I guess my problem is that I have been imposing my limitations on God (69).

On returning to China during World War II: "I'm not going back because I'm heroic. Actually, I'm a coward. But I want to go back because it's where I'm supposed to be." (98).

Every effort has been put forth to fulfill the mission of this hospital. The blind receive their sight and the halt and lame walk; the lepers are cleansed; the deaf hear and the poor have the gospel preached to them. It is our hope and prayer that the medical service in this institution shall be on that high plane befitting the glorious gospel which is preached daily within its walls.

Following Pearl Harbor and America's entrance into World War II: "We'll do what God wants us to do. It doesn't make any difference what happens to us. The only important thing is that when it does happen, we be found doing the will of God." (113).

The Superlative Servant of the Savior goes Home to His Lord

John Piper tells the story of two elderly women, medical missionaries, who died on the mission field serving the Lord Jesus. His pastoral evaluation and assessment is sobering.

As many of you know, Ruby Eliason and Laura Edwards died this week in Cameroon in a car accident – Ruby in her eighties and Laura in her seventies. Ruby gave all her life in medical missions among the poor. Laura, a doctor who practiced in

India for many years and then here in the [Twin] Cities, was giving her retirement for the bodies and the souls of the poor in Cameroon. Both died suddenly when their car went over a cliff. Was that a tragedy? Well, in one sense all death is tragic. But consider this. Ruby Eliason and Laura Edwards, at their age, could have been taking it easy here in retirement. Think of tens of thousands of retired people spending their lives in one aimless leisure after another – that is a tragedy. The fact that Jesus Christ took authority to make Ruby Eliason and Laura Edwards valiant for love and truth among the poor and lost and diseased of Cameroon when most Americans are playing their way into eternity – that is not a tragedy. And that he took them suddenly to heaven in their old age in the very moment of their love and service and sacrifice, and without long, drawn-out illnesses and without protracted and oppressive feelings of uselessness – that is not a tragedy. Rather, I say, "Give me that death, O Jesus Christ, Lord of the universe, give me that life and that ministry and that death!

The death of another medical missionary is of a similar, but not identical, nature.

On December 18, 1950, Bill Wallace completed an exhaustive day at Stout Memorial. Communist activities had been on the increase and many missionaries had been evacuated from their field assignment. Bill Wallace chose to stay and serve. Early December 19, before dawn, Chinese Communists lied their way into the clinic grounds of the hospital. Chinese soldiers ordered Bill Wallace and other workers out of their bedrooms and led them to the hospital proper. Immediately the soldiers began to accuse Dr. Wallace of being an American spy in an attempt to discredit him before the Chinese people who so deeply loved and respected him. Calmly and clearly Bill Wallace responded to their accusations by saying, "We are what we seem to be. We are doctors and nurses and hospital staff engaged in healing the suffering and sick in the name of Jesus Christ. We are here for no other reason." The soldiers went to Bill's room and returned with a small handgun. There is no question it had been planted after Bill was forced to leave his bedroom. There is no historical evidence that Bill ever owned or shot a gun in his life. However, the Communist had what they wanted. He was arrested and his nurse assistant Everley Hayes placed under house arrest. What follows is the sad and courageous account of Bill's final days from biographer Jesse Fletcher:

> Faced with wild charges of espionage, Bill was placed in a cell and left alone for some time. He was able to receive meals from the hospital and had an opportunity to tell his jailer of Jesus Christ and to preach from a cell window to two or three peasants who gathered to hear him.

> A week after his arrest, the Communists turned away the man who brought Bill's food one morning. They said he would no longer be able to receive it. That night a called meeting was held at one of the big town halls in Wuchow and all citizens of any importance were commanded to attend. There the man who had arrested the doctor arose to inform the crowd that Dr. William Wallace of the Stout Memorial Hospital had confessed to being a spy. They spoke of the gun and hinted at dark deeds the doctor had done. They asked for those who had any accusation against Dr. Wallace to come forward with their charges. None came.

What the Communists had secured from Bill was a statement concerning his name, age, length of service in China, and other factual matters. Reading it and realizing it was all true, he signed it. The Communists then typed into a blank part of the paper the statement that he had been sent to China as a secret service man by the United States government. This was the confession.

The next day, Bill was awakened early and shoved out into a courtyard where he realized for the first time he was not the only missionary being held. He recognized a Catholic sister and a bishop.

A placard with obscene and derisive accusations and charges was placed over him, and his hands were tied behind his back. With others, he was marched through the streets to the Fu River and across to the main prison halfway up the hill—that same hill to which he had gone so many times before for fellowship with his friends, the Christian and Missionary Alliance people. On the way over, shoved by a guard, he fell and badly hurt a hand that he threw out to break his fall. He received no care.

Daily, sometimes hourly, often through the night at the prison, he was awakened and brought to an interrogator's room. The world had yet to hear of brainwashing, which was to be more fully publicized after the release of the prisoner of the Korean War, but Bill Wallace began to experience it the second week of his imprisonment.

Their accusations, viciously and vehemently proclaimed, bewildered and upset him. They were shouted over and over again, growing in intensity, growing in degradation, allowing for no defense. No excuses or answers were permitted. It overwhelmed him to hear accusations of incompetence in surgery, of murdering and maiming Chinese patients, of performing illegal and obscene operations. His interrogators hinted that doctors from all over China had gathered evidence on him and were demanding his punishment. When exhausted, he was returned to the cell—a bare room with a thin pallet for protection from the damp and cold and filth of the floor.

On another day, all the foreign prisoners were gathered into an open courtyard and one by one forced to stand by a table piled high with guns, bullets, opium, radios, and other items supposed to have been confiscated in the raids in which they were arrested. Then each one was photographed behind the table. When it came Bill's turn to step up to the table, he was almost pushed into it by the guard behind him. Rudely, he was posed, with great stress being put upon his holding the aerial of a radio—to prove the spying charges.

It was obvious to the Catholic missionaries who were in prison with Bill and who were later released, that he was shaken and strained by the ordeal of interrogation. The rest of that day the prisoners were sport for a large crowd of Communist soldiers, men and women, and they suffered numerous brutalities. Toward the end of the day, one of the missionaries found an opportunity to inquire of Bill how he was holding out. With a tender smile, he replied, "All right, trusting in the Lord."

From his cell in the night, Bill sometimes cried out in agony after the battle was over. With pieces of paper and a smuggled pencil, he wrote short affirmations to try to keep his mind centered on things that he could anchor himself to. Some were Scripture passages, others simple denials of guilt, protests of innocence. He stuck these on the walls of his barren room and repeated them to himself in an effort to prepare for the next interrogation.

But each one came like a high wave. At times, he was all but overwhelmed by the interrogation. Delirium, crying, and blank periods came, but he fought on—clinging to his faith. His fellow victims, not yet subjected to the intensive brainwashing, helplessly watched this inhuman assault on one of the greatest men they had ever known. Frantically, they tried to reach him from time to time by calling through their cells. But it was a lonely battle which only Bill and the Lord—who loved him and who, somehow, in his wildest delirium he affirmed—could face.

Then something went wrong. The Communists plainly intended to brainwash their victim into an open confession, to have him repudiate publicly all that he was and all he had stood for. They thought their goal was within reach, but the tough spirit would not capitulate so easily, and his protests rang through the night.

The guards, driven by fear or perhaps guilt, came to his cell in the night with long poles and cruelly thrust them between the cell bars to jab the doctor into unconsciousness. Somebody figured wrong. For that one night the battle came to an end, and, though no one heard Bill Wallace cry, "It is finished," he offered up his spirit and brought his ministry and mission to a close. Quietly, his soul slipped from his torn body and his exhausted mind and went to be with the One he had so faithfully and resolutely served.

Bill Wallace was dead to the world, but alive forever with God.

The next morning the guards ran down the cellblock, crying that the doctor had hanged himself. Asking the two Catholic fathers imprisoned in the cell to come with them, they went into the cell where the body of the doctor was hanging from a beam by a rope of braided quilt. The guards tried to get the fathers to sign a statement that he had committed suicide. They would not do so.

Back at the hospital where the staff had waited prayerfully through all these weeks, word came to go and get the body of Dr. Wallace. Everley went with her servant and another nurse. They would not let her go into the cell, but they let the servant in, and Everley instructed him quietly to be sure to note the characteristics of the body. The facial characteristics of hanging were missing—bulging eyes, discolored face, swollen tongue. Instead, the upper torso was horribly bruised.

A cheap wooden coffin had been brought, and as soon as the body was dressed, it was put into the coffin and nailed shut by the Communist soldiers. Bill Wallace was dead. He was just 43 years old (Fletcher, 200-08).

Conclusion

Bill Wallace died on February 10, 1951. Those who worked close beside him were not allowed to see his body as the Communist attempted to hide their brutal torture of this precious servant to the

Chinese people and King Jesus. Our nation was outraged, and God's people wept all over the world. Immediately testimonies to this faithful missionary began to pop up.

A letter from Dr. Theron Rankin, executive secretary of the Foreign Mission Board.

> When God chooses someone to make a superlative witness of His love, He chooses a superlative child of His. He chose His own Son, Jesus, to make the witness on the Cross. And now it seems that He chose Bill to make this witness. To give his life in love and service for the people whom he served fits in naturally and harmoniously with Bill's life. The two things go together because he was that kind of man. His life's service among men bears out the testimony of his death. Bill's death was not the result of his being caught by a situation from which he could not escape. He deliberately chose his course with a committal that made him ready to take any consequences that might come.

From Dr. Baker James Cauthen, at the time Dr. Wallace's regional leader.

> Many things about the death of Bill Wallace make us think of the death of the Christ. The authorities were envious of his place in the hearts of people. They used falsehood in order to bring charges against him. They tried to represent him as an agent of the American government, as the Jews tried to represent Jesus as one stirring up revolt against Rome. They sought to stir up public sentiment by calling large groups of people together. They subjected him to a bitter and cruel imprisonment.

> Just as in the case of Jesus the enemies of the truth sought to discredit His testimony by declaring the disciples had come and stolen away His body, so in Wuchow the Communists stated that Dr. Wallace had died by strangling himself. This nobody believes even a moment.

By God's grace the life of this servant of the Lord Jesus has not been forgotten. There is a wonderful biography by Jesse Fletcher entitled *Bill Wallace of China*. It has been referred to throughout this chapter. A motion picture based on the book was produced. In Puchan, Korea there is the Wallace Memorial Hospital. The Baptist Student Union at the University of Tennessee Medical Center is named for Bill Wallace. In Knoxville there is also the vibrant and growing Wallace Memorial Baptist Church. However, the real memorial to this man is not in buildings, but in the hundreds of men and women who have been inspired by his life to go to the nations as missionaries for our Lord.

On January 12, 1985 a service was held at the Wallace Memorial Baptist Church as the remains of William Lindsey Wallace were returned and laid to rest in the place where he grew up. In that service Dr. James McCluskey powerfully noted:

> I cannot imagine that this congregation of believers called Wallace Memorial Baptist Church, would today have the same missions concern, outreach, love, fellowship, and joy if it was known by any other name than Wallace Memorial.

> I know that the remains of William Lindsey Wallace live on in my own life, motivating and challenging me after these more than twenty-five years as pastor of this church named in his memory.

The remains of William Lindsey Wallace are going to Costa Rica tomorrow in the life and ministry of Patricia Stooksbury as she returns there to continue her missionary service. Pat felt God's call to missions and responded to that call in the missionary environment of a church called Wallace Memorial.

The remains of William Lindsey Wallace are in Grenada, West Indies today as Charlotte and Carter Davis serve there. They experienced a call and response to serve in a spirit of missions concern cultivated in this church.

The remains of William Lindsey Wallace are in Ecuador today where Dale Maddox is completing his second year as a missionary journeyman. His missions experience came as a member of a youth missions team sent out by Wallace Memorial Baptist Church.

The remains of William Lindsey Wallace are in the lives of more than 25 young people of this church who are today either serving or preparing to serve in church-related vocations and in the lives of thousands of others who have been inspired and led by his life. The remains of William Lindsey Wallace are scattered today into the uttermost parts of the earth where missionaries give witness that Jesus Christ is Lord." (Fletcher, 252-53).

There was no funeral service for Bill Wallace. The government officials would not allow it. A grave was dug, and a nailed shut coffin was lowered into the ground. The soldiers stayed until the burial was complete and then they drove everyone away from this lonely, unmarked grave. However, it did not stay unmarked. Despite danger to themselves, friends of the kind, brave doctor collected funds for a marker and lovingly built a small monument over the solitary grave. Inscribed were seven single words that accurately captured this superlative servant of our Savior: "For to me to live is Christ."

And we know the rest of the story: "To die is gain."

The Power of a Consecrated Life: The Ministry of Lottie Moon

Romans 12:1

Lottie Moon was born Charlotte (Lottie) Diggs Moon on December 12, 1840 in Albemarle County, Virginia. She entered the world as a part of Southern aristocracy prior to the Civil War, a war that would devastate her family's fortunes. Her family's wealth was 1/40 of its pre-war value after the war ended. She would die on December 24, 1912, aboard a ship in the Japanese harbor of Kōbe. She was frail, weak and nearly starved, having just passed her 72nd birthday. She weighed no more than 50 pounds (Allen, 11).

Lottie served our Lord for 39 years on the mission field, mostly in China. Best estimates say this mighty little woman towered all of 4 feet, 3 inches. It was never said that she was beautiful, but this little lady had a certain attractiveness about her and a powerful personality that would be essential in her service on the mission field. She taught in schools for girls and made many evangelist trips into China's interior to share the gospel with women and girls. She would even preach, against her wishes, to men, because then as now there were not enough men on the mission field.

I have no doubt, having spent many months in her biography and letters, that Miss Lottie would be both amazed and embarrassed at all the fuss that is made about her each year by Southern Baptists. She knew that in 1888 Southern Baptists at her request, raised $3,315.00 to send three new female missionaries to China. She could never have imagined that in 2006, $150,178,098.06 was raised in her name. Since the inception of the Lottie Moon Christmas Offering, $2.8 billion have been raised for missions in her name. More than half of the International Mission Board's 2008 budget comes from the offering that honors her name.

Here is the power of a consecrated life, a life sold out to the Lordship of Christ, a life our Lord sovereignly chose to multiply many times over. This is the life we see outlined by the apostle Paul in Romans 12:1. Having spent 11 chapters explaining sin and salvation, sanctification and sovereignty, he now moves on that basis to address service and what I call the consecrated life.

Such a life is seen in Lottie Moon. Hers was not a perfect life, no doubt. It was, however, a powerful life; a life lived for King Jesus, and a life worthy of our careful study and attention.

Four marvelous truths emerge from this text that find a beautiful echo in the life of Lottie Moon, an echo I pray will find its sound in my life and yours.

Live a grateful life

Paul encourages us by the mercies of God, a shorthand for the many blessings he has unpacked for us in Romans 1-11. Gratitude should overwhelm every man or woman who has grasped the magnitude of sin and the majesty of salvation. Accepted in Christ by my heavenly Father, I live a life of gratitude for all that He has done for me. No request is deemed out of bounds or too great.

Lottie came to this conviction but not until she was in college. As a child her mother read to Lottie and her siblings the Bible and other religious books. One was the story of Ann Judson, the wife of Adoniram Judson and the first Baptist woman missionary from America. In December 1858, at the age of 18, Lottie placed her faith and trust in Jesus. The preacher was the famous Baptist leader John Broadus. He would also be the man who would baptize her and encourage her in her service to our Lord. In fact it was Broadus's challenge to missions that planted the seed for foreign service in her heart, though at the time a single woman going to the nations was unthinkable.

This grateful life was born of a confidence in the providence and sovereignty of God. She wrote, "I do not believe that any trouble comes upon us unless it is needed, and it seems to me that we ought to be just as thankful for sorrow as for joys." She would oft recall Broadus's prayer, "Send us affliction and trouble, blight our dearest hopes if need be, that we may learn more fully to depend on Thee" (Allen, 48).

And later in a letter to J.C. Williams, February 25, 1876, she wrote "But the work is God's and we do not fear the final results. 'The heathen shall be given to His Son for His inheritance,' and we must be content to await His own time" (Harper, 160-161).

Thus gratitude, growing of a trust in divine providence, colored Lottie's perspective on life. She needed this. When she was 12, her wealthy father died of a heart attack or stroke while on a business trip. Lottie's mother, Anna-Maria Moon, assumed family leadership.

Famine raged in north China as Lottie returned to the field in December 1877. She and other missionaries gave to relief programs and shared personally as they could to relieve the suffering.

Early in 1878 Lottie opened a girls' boarding school for higher-class Chinese. Her purpose was evangelistic: She knew the school would help her enter pupils' homes, since the exclusive citizens of Tengchow wanted little to do with "foreign devils" otherwise. God also accomplished other noble purposes.

She managed to save about a third of her pupils from the practice of binding girls' feet. The custom usually began about the time a girl would be entering school. The four small toes were bent under and bandaged and drawn toward the heel until bones broke. The suffering young women wound up with a three-inch foot and a pointed big toe. Often infection, illness and even death resulted. God was at work in surprising ways.

Lottie's life was often a life of extended loneliness. Many times she would be the only Southern Baptist missionary in northern China. Her lone companion was her Lord. But she stayed with the work God had for her. She relocated to P'ingtu in December 1885. Aided by a Chinese couple from Tengchow, she rented a four-room, dirt-floor house for $24 a year, planning to stay until summer. She ate and lived as the Chinese did. No one she knew spoke English.

She quickly adapted to the local dialect. She began visiting surrounding villages and within a few months had made 122 trips to 33 different places. She gratefully trusted our Lord in trying and difficult circumstances.

Her gratitude to God was also the basis of her challenge to folks back home to give to the work of missions. She opposed raising funds by entertainments or gimmicks. She wrote:

> I wonder how many of us really believe that it is more blessed to give than to receive. A woman who accepts that statement of our Lord Jesus Christ as a fact and not as 'impractical idealism,' will make giving a principle of her life. She will lay aside sacredly not less than one-tenth of her income or her earnings as the Lord's money, which she would no more dare touch for personal use than she would steal. How many there are among our women, alas, who imagine that because 'Jesus paid it all,' they need pay nothing, forgetting that the prime object of their salvation was that they should follow in the footsteps of Jesus Christ!

Persecution broke out against Christians in Sha-ling in 1890. Relatives of one of the first inquirers, Dan Ho-bang, tied him to a pole and beat him, but he refused to worship at ancestral tablets. A young convert, Li Show-ting, was beaten by his brothers, who tore out his hair; still, he remained steadfast in his faith. He was to become the great evangelist of north China, baptizing more than 10,000 believers.

Lottie rushed to Sha-ling and told the persecution leaders, "If you attempt to destroy his church, you will have to kill me first. Jesus gave Himself for us Christians. Now I am ready to die for Him." One of the mob prepared to kill her but was restrained. Lottie calmed the terrified believers and remained with them until the persecution waned. When the believers did not retaliate with the usual legal action, the Chinese grew in their respect of Christians and asked to hear of the new faith. The church became the strongest in north China, with its members evangelizing in nearby villages.

Let me offer one final example of her confidence in the God of providence. China's revolution broke out late in 1911. Fighting was intense around Baptist mission stations in north China. The U.S. consul asked missionaries in Hwanghsien to move to a safer port city, and they agreed — all but Lottie. When she learned Chinese hospital personnel had been left alone in Hwanghsien, she made her way safely through warring troops and took charge of the hospital, encouraging the terrified nurses and other personnel by her courage.

They resumed work, caring for the ill and wounded. When Dr. Ayers and other male missionaries risked their lives to return, they were amazed to find Lottie directing the hospital quite efficiently, as she had done for 10 days.

With the hospital in rightful hands, Lottie packed to return home, but the men warned that heavy fighting made this impossible. When she insisted, they sent word to the opposing generals that Miss Moon would be passing through at a set hour. A young missionary escorted her, and as they made their way through the battle lines, firing stopped on both sides.

Live a total life

The Bible calls us to "present our bodies." This is a personal and individual decision we all must make. It is volitional. It is to be total. "All of you, all of the time" captures the thrust of Paul's challenge. Once she came to Christ, Lottie Moon made such an agenda her life's calling and commitment.

In college she mastered Greek, Hebrew, Latin, Italian, French and Spanish. In 1861 she graduated from Albemarle Female Institute, counterpart to the University of Virginia, one of the first women in the South to receive a master's degree. Broadus would call her "the most educated (or cultured) woman in the South" (Allen, 39).

During the Civil War she and her sisters Colie and Mollie nursed soldiers at Charlottesville as well as her brother Orie back home.

Prior to leaving for China, she taught Sunday School near Viewpoint to both black and white children.

Lottie felt her call to China "as clear as a bell" in February 1873, after hearing a sermon on missions at First Baptist Church in Cartersville, Georgia. Lottie left the service to go to her room, where she prayed all afternoon.

On July 7, 1873, the Foreign Mission Board appointed Charlotte Digges Moon as a missionary. She was asked to join her sister who actually had preceded her to the mission field in Tengchow. About to sail from San Francisco, Lottie received word that Baptist women in Cartersville would support her. There was no Cooperative Program at this time. It would not come into existence until 1925!

In village after village she would travel to speak from early morning to late evening, from the kang, on the street, in the yard of dirty homes, traveling in shentzes or riding donkeys, in the heat and dust of summer or wintry rain and snow. She was constantly in contact with the people, continually at risk of exposure to smallpox and other diseases. Yet she suppressed her craving for cultured life and conversation and her Southern tastes — all for the cause of Christ. "As I wander from village to village," she said, "I feel it is no idle fancy that the Master walks beside me, and I hear His voice saying gently, 'I am with you always, even unto the end.'"

She found strength in prayer and Bible reading and in devotional classics. She often wrote quotations from spiritual writings in the margin of her Bible or devotional books. One favorite was from Francis de Sales: "Go on joyously as much as you can, and if you do not always go on joyously, at best go on courageously and confidently."

It was Lottie who suggested to Dr. H.A. Tupper, head of the Mission Board, that the board follow the pattern of some other mission groups and provide for a year of furlough after 10 years on the field. The board eventually adopted such a policy, but not until several missionaries in China died prematurely and others returned home in broken health.

Lottie repeatedly struggled with the tragic fact that more did not answer the call to missions, especially men. What follows are the texts of letter she wrote to Tupper and others of the need (all letters are addressed to Tupper unless otherwise noted):

November 1, 1873:
What we need in China is more workers. The harvest is very great, the laborers, oh! so few. Why does the Southern Baptist church lag behind in this great work?...I think your idea is correct, that a young man should ask himself not if it is his duty to go to the heathen, but if he may dare stay at home. The command is so plain: "Go." (Harper, 7).

April 27, 1874:
Oh that we had active and zealous men who would go far and wide scattering books and tracts and preaching the word to the vast multitudes of this land." (Harper, 80).

November 4, 1875:

"I write today moved by feelings which come over me constantly when I go out on country trips. "The harvest is plenteous, the laborers are few….What we find missionaries can do in the way of preaching the gospel even in the immediate neighborhood of this city, is but as the thousandth part of a drop in the bucket compared with what should be done. I do not pretend to aver that there is any spiritual interest among the people. They literally "sit in darkness & in the shadow of death." The burden of our words to them is the folly and sin of idol worship. We are but doing pioneer work, but breaking up the soil in which we believe others shall sow a bountiful crop. But, as in the natural soil, four or five laborers cannot possibly cultivate a radius of twenty miles, so cannot we, a mission of five people, do more than make a beginning of what should be done….But is there no way to arouse the churches on this subject? We missionaries find it in our hearts to say to them in all humility, "Now then we are ambassadors for Christ; as though God did beseech you by us, we pray you, in Christ's stead," to remember the heathen. We implore you to send us help. Let not these heathen sink down into eternal death without one opportunity to hear that blessed Gospel which is to you the source of all joy & comfort. The work that constantly presses upon us is greater than time or strength permit us to do." (Harper, 17).

April 14, 1876:

There was a large crowd pretty soon in attendance, so many that the hall would not hold them & they adjourned to the yard. I hope you won't think me desperately unfeminine, but I spoke to them all, men, women, and children, pleading with them to turn from their idolatry to the True & Living God. I should not have dared to remain silent with so many souls before me sunk in heathen darkness. (Harper, 32).

October 10, 1878:
Odd that with five hundred Baptist preachers in the state of Virginia we must rely on a Presbyterian minister to fill a Baptist pulpit. I wonder how these things look in Heaven: they certainly look very queer in China. But then we Baptists are a great people as we never tire of saying at our associations and Conventions, & possibly our way of doing things is the best! (Harper, 78).

November 11, 1878:
But how inadequate our force! Here is a province of thirty million souls & Southern Baptists can only send one man & three women to tell them the story of redeeming love. Oh! That my words could be as a trumpet call stirring the hearts of my brethren & sisters to pray, to labor, to give themselves to this people. "But," some will say, "we must have results, else interest flags." I have seen the husbandman go forth in the autumn to plow the fields; later, I have seen him scatter the seed broadcast; anon, the tiny green shoots came up scarcely visible at first; then the snows of winter fell concealing them for weeks; spring brought its fructifying rains, its genial sunshine, & lo! in June the golden harvest. We are now, a very, very few feeble workers, scattering the grain broadcast according as time & strength permit. God will give the harvest; doubt it not. But the laborers are so few. Where we have four, we should have not less than one hundred. Are these wild words? They would not seem so were the church of God

awake to her high privileges & her weighty responsibilities."
(Harper, 83)

An "Open Letter" to the Religious Herald, **no date:**
I am trying honestly to do the work that could fill the hands of
three or four women, and in addition must do much work that
ought to be done by young men ... Our dilemma-to do men's
work or to sit silent at religious services conducted by men
just emerging from heathenism.

January 8, 1889:
There is so much work to be done, too, that ought to be done
by men. A young woman could not do the work & retain the
respect of Chinese men ... While I do not a little for the men
& the boys, I do not feel bound to stay on their account. Still,
I must add that the work is suffering & will continue to suffer
in that department for want of a man living on the spot.

September 1877, to the Foreign Mission Journal:
In the vast continent of Africa, we have one white missionary
& one colored. In Japan we have—not one. In China we have
at present eight missionaries. Putting the population of China
at four hundred million, this gives one missionary for fifty
million people. Yet, we call ourselves Missionary Baptists.

Our Lord says, "Go ye into all the world & preach the gospel
to every creature." Are we obeying this command?"

January 1888, to the Foreign Mission Journal:
The needs of these people press upon my soul, and I cannot be
silent. It is grievous to think of these human souls going down
to death without even one opportunity of hearing the name of
Jesus. People talk vaguely about the heathen, picturing them
as scarcely human, or at best, as ignorant barbarians. If they

could live among them as I do, they would find in the men much to respect and admire; in the women and girls they would see many sweet and loving traits of character. They would feel, pressing upon their heart and conscience, the duty of giving the gospel to them. It does seem strange that when men and women can be found willing to risk life—or, at least, health and strength—in order that these people may hear the gospel, that Christians withhold the means to send them. Once more I urge upon the consciences of my Christian brethren and sisters the claims of these people among whom I dwell. Here I am working alone in a city of many thousand inhabitants, with numberless villages clustered around or stretching away in the illuminate distance: how many can I reach?

It fills one with sorrow to see these people so earnest in their worship of false gods, seeking to work out their salvation by supposed works of merit, with no one to tell them of a better way. Then, to remember the wealth hoarded in Christian coffers! The money lavished on fine dresses and costly living! Is it not time for Christian men and women to return to the simplicity of earlier times? Should we not press it home upon our consciences that the sole object of our conversion was not the salvation of our own souls, but that we might become co-workers with our Lord and Master in the conversion of the world?

May 1889 to the Foreign Mission Journal:
One cannot help asking sadly, why is love of gold more potent than love of souls? The number of men mining and prospecting for gold in Shantung is more than double the number of men representing Southern Baptists! What a lesson for Southern Baptists to ponder!

Live a sacrificial life

"A living sacrifice." The phrase sounds odd, oxymoronic. And yet is its meaning not plain? The consecrated life is both alive and dead at the same time. When I am sold out to Christ there are times in which I am active, vibrant, alive. Since I am sold out to Christ there are some things that once thrilled me, delighted me and consumed me but I am now dead to them. I know them but I am dead to them. They are not my life, my passion, any longer. It is now all about Christ and His calling upon my life. Such a life the Bible says is holy and acceptable to God.

The little aristocratic lady from Virginia lived such a life on many levels. Listen to her spirited correspondence to Dr. Tupper, dated November 11, 1878, concerning living conditions on the field:

> Possibly you may have noticed throughout this letter that I have made frequent illusions to physical discomforts & to weariness of mind & body. I have always been ashamed in writing of missionary work to dwell upon physical hardships & then too we get so accustomed to take them as a matter of course that it does not occur to us to speak of them save in a general way. In this letter I have purposely departed from my usual reticence upon such matters because I know that there are some who, in their pleasant homes in America, without any real knowledge of the facts, declare that the days of missionary hardships are over. To speak in the open air, in a foreign tongue, from six to eleven times a day, is no trifle. The fatigue of travel is something. The inns are simply the acme of discomfort. If anyone fancies that sleeping on brick beds, in rooms with dirt floor, with walls blackened by the smoke

of generations, —the yard to these quarters being also the stable yard, & the stable itself being in three feet of the door of your apartment, —if anyone thinks all this agreeable, then I wish to declare most emphatically that as a matter of taste I differ. If anyone thinks he would like this constant contact with what an English writer has called the "Great Unwashed," I must still say that from experience I find it unpleasant. If anyone thinks that constant exposure to the risk of small-pox & other contagious diseases against which the Chinese take no precautions whatever, is just the most charming thing in life, I must still beg leave to say that I shall continue to differ in opinion. In a word, let him come out & try it. A few days roughing it as we ladies do habitually will convince the most skeptical. There is a passage from Farrar's "Life of Christ," which recurred forcibly to my mind during this recent country tour. "From early dawn … to late evening in whatever house He had selected for His nightly rest, the multitude came crowding about him, not respecting his privacy, not allowing for his weariness, eager to see Him … There was no time even to eat bread. Such a life is not only to the last degree trying & fatiguing, but to a refined & high strung nature … This incessant publicity, this apparently illimitable toil becomes simply maddening unless the spirit be sustained." He was the Son of God but we missionaries, we are only trying in a very poor way to walk in His footsteps & this "boundless sympathy & love" is of the divine & not the human.

A few words more & I have done. We are astonished at the wide door opened us for work. We have such access to the people, to their hearts & homes as we could not have dared to hope two years ago.

But there is one living sacrifice Lottie made that I especially wish to draw to your attention. Miss Moon never married, though she did receive a proposal that she would turn down. There was a brilliant Hebrew and Old Testament scholar named Crawford Toy. Some have called him the "crown jewel" of Southern Seminary as he was one of its earliest and, without question, brightest young faculty members. Though all of the precise details are not clear, a general outline of the relationship between Dr. Toy and Miss Moon can be sketched.

They met when she was a student at Albemarle Female Institute and he was an assistant to the principal, a noted educator name John Hart. At the time Lottie "was considered a brain and a heretic." It appears Lottie and Crawford developed something more than a student-pupil relationship during her time there.

Toy committed himself to be a missionary. Lottie would make the same commitment a few years later. Set to sail for the mission field in 1860, Toy mysteriously did not go.

In 1870, Toy returned from studying in Germany to teach at Southern Seminary. He had ingested the liberal historical criticism popular in European universities.

Around 1876 Lottie returned from China accompanying her sister Edmonia ("Eddie") who had suffered an emotional breakdown while on the field. At this time she and Crawford Toy saw each other and apparently rekindled their relationship. This would continue in some measure until 1882.

Controversy on the mission field led Lottie to consider leaving China and returning to America to marry Toy. Some Moon scholars believe the proposed marriage may have occurred earlier when Toy was planning to go to Japan and Lottie was beginning to sense God's call to missions as well.

The wedding never took place. According to Toy's own family, the engagement was broken because of religious differences. It appears Toy's slide into theological liberalism and backtracking on going to the mission field led Lottie to break off their engagement. Toy would go to Harvard and die a Unitarian. Lottie would remain in China and die alone. Lottie was later asked by a young relative, "Aunt Lottie, have you ever been in love?" She answered, "Yes, but God had first claim on my life, and since the two conflicted, there could be no question about the results." (Allen, 139).

In 1888 Lottie would forcibly address the "new theology" of Toy and others that was being much discussed in America. With keen insight she saw it would be fatal to the mission enterprise. She used the occasion to critique its danger and chide her fellow Baptists for their missionary indifference. Her biographer Catherine Allen summarizes her prophetic call:

> **Although she was committed primarily to teaching the women, and next to dealing with the children, she could not keep the men from listening from adjoining rooms. In the case of Sha-ling, the men were the primary inquirers. Each evening and on Sunday she would conduct a service of worship. In a little low-ceilinged room, lit by wicks in saucers of bean oil, the worshipers would gather. A makeshift screen of grain stalks divided the crown of men from women. With Miss Moon's direction, the semi-heathen men would lead singing, read Scripture, rehearse the catechism, and pray. Miss Moon would sometimes comment on the Scripture. If Mrs. Crawford were present, she would be willing to deliver what amounted to a sermon.**

With such ready response to the gospel, Miss Moon was incredulous that Southern Baptist preachers and young women were not flocking to China. From Pingtu she quickened the flow of appeals. Now she turned to shaming, chiding, flattering — any tactic to get the attention of the apathetic Baptists. In one appeal she concluded that the folks back home had all adopted the "new theology" the Baptist editors had been criticizing ever since the Toy episode. One had predicted that "new theology" would quench the missionary spirit.

'I conclude that the large majority of Southern Baptists have adopted this 'new theology," she wrote. 'Else, why this strange indifferences to missions? Why these scant contributions …. The needs of these people press upon my soul, and I cannot be silent. People talk vaguely about the heathen, picturing them as scarcely human, or at best, as ignorant barbarians. If they could live among them as I do, they would find in the men much to respect and admire; in the women and girls they would see many sweet and loveable traits of character …. Here I am working alone in a city of many thousand inhabitants with numberless villages. How many can I reach?' (Allen, 172).

Live a worshipful life

The consecrated life is what Paul calls "your reasonable service" (NKJV). Other English translations render it "your spiritual act of worship" (NIV); "your spiritual service of worship" (NASV); "your spiritual worship" (ESV; HCSB).

Paul's point is that a consecrated life is a worshipping life. It is a constant and continuous life of service lived out 24 hours a day, seven days a week in thanksgiving for all that we enjoy in Christ. It is a life truly satisfied in God, His good, His glory. Such satisfaction is evidence in Lottie's life.

In her Bible Lottie wrote, "Words fail to express my love for this holy Book, my gratitude for its author, for His love and goodness. How shall I thank him for it?" (Allen, 160).

Lottie also had a great confidence in the sovereignty of God and a dependence on the work of the Holy Spirit. She said, "I have a firm conviction that I am immortal 'til my work is done." (Allen, 294). She also wrote, "I feel my weakness and inability to accomplish anything without the aid of the Holy Spirit. Make special prayer for the outpouring of the Holy Spirit in P'ingtu, that I may be clothed with power from on high by the indwelling of the Spirit in my heart." (Allen, 160).

She further had a great love for the lost, which propelled her on in this worshipful life she lived. She said, "We must go out and live among them, manifesting the gentle, loving spirit of our Lord. We need to make friends before we can hope to make converts." (Allen, 160).

During the 1890's Lottie set a goal to visit 200 villages every 3 months. She would write, "I have never found mission work more enjoyable …. I constantly thank God He has given me a work I love so much."

As an aside, Lottie adopted traditional Chinese dress and learned their customs. Not only did she serve them, she identified with them, even in her death. The following letter was printed in the August 1887

Foreign Mission Journal:

> I feel that I would gladly give my life to working among such a people and regard it as a joy and privilege. Yet, to women who may think of coming, I would say, count well the cost. You must give up all that you hold dear, and live a life that is, outside of your work, narrow and contracted to the last degree. If you really love the work, it will atone for all you give up, and when your work is ended and you go Home, to see the Master's smile and hear his voice of welcome will more than repay your toils amid the heathen.

In the year of her death, 2,358 persons were baptized in her field of service, nearly doubling the Baptist population in the area (Allen, 292).

Her worshipful life also grew out of a tremendous love for Jesus. In a May 10, 1879 letter to Tupper, she wrote:

> Recall for a moment the thoughts that crowd upon the mind. This ancient continent of Asia whose soil you are treading was the chosen theatre for the advent of the Son of God. In a rush of grateful emotion there came to your mind the lines of that grand old hymn the "Dies Irae," "Seeking me Thy worn feet hasted, On the cross Thy soul death tasted," and your heart is all aglow with longing to bear to others the priceless gift that you have received, that thus you may manifest your thankfulness & love to the giver. He "went about doing good"; in a humble manner you are trying to walk in his footsteps. As you wend your way from village to village, you feel it is no idle fancy that the Master walks beside you and you hear his voice saying gently, "Lo! I am with you always even unto the

end." And the soul makes answer in the words of St. Bernard, that holy man of God, "Lord Jesus, thou are home and friends and fatherland to me." Is it any wonder that as you draw near to the villages a feeling of exultation comes over you? That your heart goes up to God in glad thanksgiving that he has so trusted you as to commit to your hands this glorious gospel that you may convey its blessings to those who still sit in darkness? When the heart is full of such joy, it is no effort to speak to the people: you could not keep silent if you would. Mere physical hardships sink into merited insignificance. What does one care for comfortless inns, hard beds, hard fare, when all around is a world of joy and glory and beauty? (Harper, 89).

On her deathbed, speaking to her friend and fellow missionary Cynthia Miller, Lottie said, "Jesus is here right now. You can pray now that he will fill my heart and stay with me. For when Jesus comes in, he drives out all evil .... Jesus loves me. This I know, for the Bible tells me so. Little ones to him belong. They are weak, but he is strong. Do you know this song, Miss Miller?"

Miss Miller would write following her death, "It is infinitely touching that those who work hardest and make the most sacrifices for the Master should suffer because those in the homeland fail to give what is needed."

Dr. T. W. Ayers said, "[Lottie Moon] is one woman who will have her crown covered with stars. She is one of the most unselfish saints God ever made." (Harper, 447).

Conclusion

Lottie Moon died at age 72, a frail 50 pounds, refusing to eat that her food portion might go to others. Her remains were cremated at Yokohama, Japan on December 26. Personal effects consisted of one steamer trunk. The executor of her estate sold all of her personal property and cleared her bank account of $254 in inflated local currency. He wrote with a broken heart, "The heiress of Viewmount did not have enough estate to pay her way back to Virginia." (Allen, 288). She had given all she had to King Jesus. Twenty years following her death, Chinese women in remote villages would ask, "when will the Heavenly Book visitor come again?" Their testimony about her was, "how she loved us."

One year following Lottie's death, Agnes Osborne suggested the annual Women's Missionary Union foreign missions offering being taken as a living memorial to Lottie Moon, noting that Lottie's suggestions launched the offering to begin with. In 1918 Annie Armstrong, for whom Southern Baptists' home missions offering was established, said, "Miss Moon is the one who suggested the Christmas offering for foreign missions. She showed us the way in so many things. Wouldn't it be appropriate to name the offering in her memory?" The issue was settled and the rest is history. (Allen, 293).

Following her death fellow missionaries came in possession of her Bible. On the flyleaf words were found which she had penned that remain to this day a perpetual encouragement to those who go for Christ to the nations, "O, that I could consecrate myself, soul and body, to his service forever; O, that I could give myself up to him, so as never more to attempt to be my own or to have any will or affection improper for those conformed to him." (Allen, 139). She did. Will you?

*Sources:
Catherine Allen, *The New Lottie Moon Story*
Keith Harper, *Send the Light: Lottie Moon's Letters and Other Writings*

Let All the Nations Give God Glory!: A Passion in the Life & Martyrdom of Jim Elliot

❧

Psalm 96

A true and genuine movement of our great God will cause the church to look *up* to heaven; catching a vision of His greatness; *in* to view our own desperate sinfulness apart from His grace; and *out* to see the lostness of the nations cut off from His goodness.

Such a movement of God engulfed and baptized the man and missionary Jim Elliot who would passionately seek to extend the glory of God among the nations. He would do this only to see his earthly life, and those of his four faithful companions, end in martyrdom among the Auca Indians in Ecuador at the age of 29, the same life span God granted to another missionary by the name of David Brainerd (1718-1747).

Neither Jim's life, or indeed any of these lives, was a loss. On the contrary, more of the nations were added to give God glory because of their radical devotion to "the Lord [who] is great and greatly to be praised." (v.4).

I think James Boice captures the full impact of Psalm 96 when he says, "it is a joyful hymn to the God of Israel as king and an invitation to the nations of the world to join Israel in praising Him. It is also a prophecy of a future day when God will judge the entire world in righteousness" (*Psalms,* vol. 2, 782).

It is this type of theology that drove Jim Elliot to give his life as a missionary, that inspired him to pray, "Oh that God would make us dangerous" (*Shadow of the Almighty,* 79). It is this kind of theology that will not let you be satisfied with a shallow, impotent, useless and comfortable Christianity. It requires more! It inspires more!

This psalm has 4 major movements that focus on the desires of God in relation to the nations. What does He want? What does He rightly deserve?

God Desires that the Nations Praise Him
Psalm 96:1-3

God is identified as the LORD (Yahweh) 11 times in this psalm. Here all the earth (v.11) is invited to praise Him. Three aspects of praise are specified.

We Should Sing a New Song, Psalm 96:1

Three times we are called to "sing to the Lord" in vs. 1-2. Here it is said we should sing "a new song." The new song is the good news of His salvation "from day to day" (v. 2). It looks back to His mighty acts of deliverance, especially the Exodus, but it also looks forward to the greatest act of salvation in Jesus Christ, witnessed climatically in

Revelation 5:9-10 and 14:3-5:

> And they sang a new song, saying "You are worthy to take the scroll, and to open its seals; for you were slain, and have redeemed us to God by your blood out of every tribe and tongue and people and nation, and have made us kings and priests to our God; and we shall reign on the earth.

> They sang as it were a new song before the throne, before the four living creatures, and the elders; and no one could learn that song except the hundred and forty-four thousand who were redeemed from the earth. These are the ones who were not defiled with women, for they are virgins. These are the ones who follow the Lamb wherever He goes. These were redeemed from among men, being firstfruits to God and to the Lamb. And in their mouth was found no deceit, for they are without fault before the throne of God.

The new song of salvation will be sung by all the nations!

We Should Proclaim His Salvation, Psalm 96:2

The three imperatives "sing" are paralleled by three additional imperatives in vs. 2-3: "bless, proclaim, declare." Singing to the Lord we bless His name, we honor and give glory to the name of the LORD (Yahweh). We do this as we "proclaim the good news of His salvation from day to day." The idea is that not a day goes by, not a moment passes, that our hearts and minds and mouths are not occupied with the wonder of His salvation (v.3).

We Should Declare His Glory, Psalm 96:3

The new song (v.1) and good news (v.2) of the Lord's salvation demands a universal, worldwide declaration. "The glory of this God must be declared among the nations and His wonders among all peoples."

Eugene Peterson paraphrases it this way in *The Message*, "Shout the news of His victory from sea to sea, take the news of His glory to the lost, news of His wonders to one and all!"

This was the passion of Philip James Elliot. Born in 1926 in Portland, Oregon, God blessed him with a father who was an itinerant evangelist. While he was not an educated man, Fred Elliot's love and devotion to Christ would significantly shape the life of his son. Of his father he would write in a letter to his future wife Elisabeth, whom he called Betty:

Betty, I blush to think of things I have said, as if I knew something about what Scripture teaches. I know nothing. My father's religion is of a sort which I have seen nowhere else. His theology is wholly undeveloped, but so real and practical a thing that it shatters every 'system' of doctrine I have seen. He cannot define theism, but he knows God. We've had some happy times together, and I cannot estimate what enrichment a few months' working with him might do for me, practically and spiritually.

His journal adds this, dated January 29: "When I think of how far he has gone into the secret riches of the Father's purposes in Christ, I am shamed to silence. O Lord, let me learn tenderness and silence in my spirit, fruits of Thy knowledge. Burn, burden, break me." (S.A., 90-91).

Jim's home was often visited by missionaries, and at about the age of 8 he trusted Jesus as his Savior. As a teen the thought of being a missionary was already in his heart. It is never too early to consider such life decisions! He was a fine athlete who saw sports as a helpful way of preparing his body for the rigors of the mission field.

He enrolled at Wheaton College in 1948, joined the wrestling team, began speaking to youth groups, began journaling in his junior year, and met Betty.

It was in June 1950 that Jim's passion to see the nations praise the Lord Jesus saw his heart drawn to the remote and greatly feared Huaorani tribe in Ecuador, known in that day as the "Aucas." Two written pieces capture what God had placed in his heart. The first is a letter to his parents dated August 8, 1950:

> Surely those who know the great passionate heart of Jehovah must deny their own loves to share in the statement of His. Consider the call from the Throne above, Go ye, and from round about, Come over and help us, and even the call from the damned souls below, Send Lazarus to my brothers, that they come not to this place. Impelled, then, by these voices, I dare not stay home while Quichuas perish. So what if the well-fed church in the homeland needs stirring? They have the Scriptures, Moses, and the Prophets, and a whole lot more. Their condemnation is written on their bank books and in the dust on their Bible covers. American believers have sold their lives to the service of Mammon, and God has His rightful way of dealing with those who succumb to the spirit of Laodicea.

The second is a journal entry dated July 26, 1952: "Oh for a faith that sings!...Lord God, give me a faith that will take sufficient quiver out of me so that I may sing! Over the Aucas, Father I want to sing."

God Desires that the Nations Fear Him
Psalm 96:4-6

A right theology of God will lead to a healthy reverence, even fear and awe of Him. He will not be insulted as "the man upstairs" or "my buddy and pal." "J.C. is my homeboy" will be dismissed for the dishonoring and disrespectful sham that it is. No, this God is the omnipotent, omniscient, omnipresent sovereign of the universe who is coming "to judge the earth...the world with righteousness" (v.13).

The psalmist, therefore, says fear Him! Why? Two reasons are given.

First, we should fear Him because He is a great God. Our God is a great God and greatly (NIV, "most worthy") to be praised. He is to be feared above all the other gods. Why? Because the gods of the peoples are idols, false gods, imposters, no gods at all. They are scattered around the globe enslaving millions to false idols and false systems of religion that are an expressway to hell.

The Lord is great and they are not. He saves and they damn. The Lord is really something and they are really nothing. The Lord made everything. They have made nothing.

Second, we should fear Him because He is a glorious God. Four marvelous affirmations are made of the great redeemer and Creator God in v. 6. These are truths the nations need to know.

Honor (NASV, "splendor") is before Him, radiating from His person. Majesty is before Him, flooding forth from Him. Strength is found in His sanctuary, His royal residence. Beauty is found in His sanctuary, His kingly court. Standing before the great God like "throne room attendants," honor, majesty, strength and beauty bear witness to the God who is awesome and like no other.

Elisabeth Elliot said of her husband, "Jim's aim was to know God" (S.A., 9). Jim himself would write, "Lord, make my way prosperous, not that I achieve high station, but that my life may be an exhibit to the value of knowing God" (S.A., 11). Jim Elliot saw our God for who He is and a holy reverence and fear attended him while at Wheaton and drove him to take the gospel to the Aucas.

Note these journal entries:

July 15, 1948
How like Orpah I am – prone to kiss, to display full devotion and turn away; how unlike Ruth, cleaving and refusing to part except at death (1:14-17). Eternal Lover, make Thou Thyself inseparable from my unstable soul. Be Thou the object bright and fair to fill and satisfy the heart. My hope to meet Thee in the air, and nevermore from Thee to part!

October 27, 1948
Sense a great need of my Father tonight. Have feelings of what Dr. Jaarsma [philosophy professor at Wheaton] calls "autonomous man" in another context. I do not feel needy enough. Sufficiency in myself is a persistent thought, though I try to judge it. Lord Jesus, Tender Lover of this brute soul, wilt Thou make me weak? I long to understand Thy sufficiency and my inadequacy, and how can I sense this except in experience? So, Lord, Thou knowest what I am able to bear. Send trouble that I might know peace; send anxiety that I might know rest in Thee. Send hard things that I may learn to rely on Thy dissolving them. Strange askings, and I do not know what I speak, but "my desire is toward Thee" – anything that will intensify and make me tender, Savior. I desire to be

like Thee, Thou knowest.

October 28, 1948

Wonderful season of intercession...tonight. "At thy right hand are pleasures..." (Pss. 16:11). Prayed a strange prayer today. I covenanted with my Father that He would do either of two things-either glorify Himself to the utmost in me, or slay me. By His grace I shall not have His second best. For He heard me, I believe, so that now I have nothing to look forward to but a life of sacrificial sonship (that's how thy Savior was glorified, my soul) or heaven soon. Perhaps tomorrow. What a prospect!

November 1, 1948

Son of Man, I feel it would be best if I should be taken now to Thy throne. I dread causing Thee shame at Thy appearing (Mark 8:38). Father, take my life, yea, my blood if Thou wilt, and consume it with Thine enveloping fire. I would not save it, for it is not mine to save. Have it, Lord, have it all. Pour out my life as an oblation for the world. Blood is only of value as it flows before Thine altar (S.A., 247).

Here we find the words, the heart, of a man who rightly feared the Lord. How strange his words sound to the convenient Christianity that has engulfed our churches. We would say he is a fanatic. What would Jesus say? What he had we desperately need. What he had must be shared.

God Desires that the Nations Worship Him
Psalm 96:7-9

Warren Wiersbe says, "Praise means looking up, but worship

means bowing down" (*Bible Exposition Commentary,* 264). It means to acknowledge and ascribe to God His worth and value by humbling ourselves before Him and submitting to His will for our lives.

Three times in this third stanza we are commanded to "give" or "ascribe" glory to God, a glory that rightly belongs only to Him and a glory that should come from "the families of the nations" (NIV). These words are almost identical to the beginning of Psalm 29. There it is the angels who are called to worship the Lord. Here it is the nations. What are we to give to the great and greatly to be praised God?

First, we are to give Him honor, according to vs. 7-8. All the nations are summoned to give the Lord acknowledgement of His glory and strength, glory due to the name of Yahweh, the name above all names that Philippians 2:9-11 informs us, is the name of Jesus. The honor He rightly deserves is proven by an offering that is brought into His presence. The apostle Paul will speak of our giving our bodies as an offering, as "living sacrifices" to King Jesus (Romans 12:1).

Second, we are to acknowledge His holiness, according to v. 9. We honor Him because of the beauty or splendor of His holiness, His moral perfection, His utter transcendence and greatness. In light of our sinfulness and depravity, our finitude and creaturliness, we and all the earth rightly tremble before such a God. No doing "the wave" before this God. No "three cheers for Jesus" from those who see Him for who He is and see us for who we are without Him.

Again, I believe there is much to learn from the life and martyrdom of Jim Elliot, in his own words from his journal.

> **November 6, 1948**
> "Forgive me for being so ordinary while claiming to know so extraordinary a God."

September 19, 1948

To worship in truth is not sufficient, that is to worship in
true form. There must be exercise of the spirit; the new man
must be stirred to action; we must have spiritual worship.
Philippians 3:3: We have mention of emotional worship
– rejoicing in soul as well as exercising in spirit. Paul has
spoken of rejoicing in the Gospel's furtherance (1:18); in the
sending of Epaphroditus (2:25), and now he says, 'Finally,
rejoice in the Lord' (3:1). Not in fellowship or in privileges,
but in the Lord. 'Delight thyself also in the Lord' (Ps. 37:4).
Then Romans 12:1, 2 gives us rational worship, involving
the presentation of our bodies. Yea, Lord, make me a true
worshiper!

September 20

2 Chronicles 20. I cannot explain the yearnings of my heart
this morning. Cannot bring myself to study or to pray for
any length of time. Oh, what a jumble of cross-currented
passions I am – a heart so deceitful it deceives itself. May
Christ satisfy my thirst, may the river Rock pour out Himself
to me in this desert place. Nothing satisfies - not nature, or
fellowship with any, but only my Eternal Lover. Ah, how cold
my heart is toward Him. But "our eyes are upon Thee" (v. 12).
Possibility of seeing Betty again brings back wistful thoughts.
*[Betty is Elisabeth whom he would eventually marry. They would serve
together in Ecuador and have one child together, Valerie].* **How I hate
myself for such weakness! Is not Christ enough, Jim? What
need you more — a woman — in His place? Nay, God forbid.
I shall have Thee, Lord Jesus. Thou didst buy me, now I must
buy Thee. Thou knowest how reluctant I am to pay, because I
do not value Thee sufficiently. I am Thine at terrible cost to**

Thyself. Now Thou must become mine — as Thou didst not attend to the price, neither would I.

August 16, 1954
Because O God, from Thee comes all, because from Thine own mouth has entered us the power to breathe, from Thee the sea of air in which we swim and the unknown nothingness that stays it over us with unseen bonds; because Thou gavest us from heart of love so tender, mind so wise and hand so strong, Salvation; because Thou are Beginning, God, I worship Thee.

Because Thou are the end of every way, the goal of man; because to Thee shall come of every people respect and praise; their emissaries find Thy throne their destiny; because Ethiopia shall stretch out her hands to Thee, babes sing Thy praise; because Thine altar gives to sparrows shelter, sinners peace, and devils fury; because "to Thee shall all flesh come"; because Thou art Omega. Praise.

Because Thou sure art set to justify that Son of Thine and wilt in time make known just who He is and soon will send Him back to show Himself; because the Name of Jesus has been laughingly nailed upon a cross and is just now on earth held very lightly and Thou wilt bring that Name to light; because, O God of righteousness, Thou wilt do right by my Lord, Jesus Christ, I worship Thee.

God Desires that the Nations Enjoy Him
Psalm 96:10-13

John Piper loves to say, "God is most glorified in us when we are most satisfied in Him." In other words God wants us, He wants the nations, to enjoy Him. We could spend all of eternity listing the reasons we should enjoy our great God, but Psalm 96 highlights two reasons that shine like the sun announcing the glory and goodness of God.

First, we enjoy Him because He is a sovereign King, according to vs. 10-12. The nations must hear that this God reigns, He rules sovereignly over the whole earth. He made it ("the world is firmly established") and He maintains it ("it shall not be moved"). He's got the whole world in His hands.

He shall judge the peoples righteously. No one will ever point a finger at God and say, "You were not fair. You did me wrong." You cannot bribe this God. He plays no favorites in judging the nations. Here is one judge you can always count on to do the right thing.

In light of all this enjoy Him!

Let the heavens rejoice.

Let the earth be glad.

Let the sea roar and all that is in it.

Let the field be joyful and all that is in it.

In antiphonal response "all the trees of the forest will rejoice before Yahweh, before the Lord."

Second, we enjoy Him because He is a righteous King, according to verse 13. This psalm ends on an eschatological note, a note of hope for those who love and enjoy Him, a note of warning for those who reject His rightful lordship over their lives. He is coming to judge the earth. He is coming to judge the world with righteousness. He is coming to judge the peoples with His truth. What does this look like? Revelation 19:11-16 has the answer:

Now I saw heaven opened, and behold, a white horse. And He who sat on him was called Faithful and True, and in righteousness He judges and makes war. His eyes were like a flame of fire, and on His head were many crowns. He had a name written that no one knew except Himself. He was clothed with a robe dipped in blood, and His name is called The Word of God. And the armies in heaven, clothed in fine linen, white and clean, followed Him on white horses. Now out of His mouth goes a sharp sword, that with it He should strike the nations. And He Himself will rule them with a rod of iron. He Himself treads the winepress of the fierceness and wrath of Almighty God. And He has on His robe and on His thigh a name written: KING OF KINGS AND LORD OF LORDS.

Conclusion

Jim Elliot wrote in a letter to his family, "Remember you are immortal until your work is done. But don't let the sands of time get into the eyes of your vision to reach those who still sit in darkness. They simply must hear." (S.A.,81). Just before he left for the last time Elisabeth asked Jim that if they were attacked by the Aucas, would they use their guns? Jim's response was clear and certain: "We will not use our guns!" When Elisabeth asked why he simply said, "Because we are ready for heaven, but they are not."

On January 8, 1956, Jim Elliot, along with Ed McCully, Roger Youderian, Pete Fleming and Nate Saint, waited hopefully for another meeting with the Auca or Huaorani Indians, having had several friendly encounters in previous days. However, a group of 10 Huaorani men attacked the five missionaries and brutally murdered them. Jim Elliot's mutilated body was found downstream in the river. There was no funeral, no tombstone for a memorial. However, on resurrection day the glorified bodies of these champions for Jesus will rise from the dirt of Ecuador! Jim left behind his wife Elizabeth and a baby girl. They had been married less than three years.

On January 30, 1956, *Life* published a 10-page article on the martyrdom of these men entitled, "Go ye and preach the Gospel' — five devout Americans in remote Ecuador follow this precept and are killed."

Our nation was shocked and Christians all over the world wept. Jim would have been embarrassed by this. In a letter to his parents dated June 23, 1947, he wrote, "Missionaries are very human folks, just doing what they are asked. Simply a bunch of nobodies trying to exalt Somebody" (S.A., 46).

And in a letter to his mother dated August 16, 1948, Jim wrote, "Oh what a privilege to be made a minister of the things of the 'happy God.' I only hope that He will let me preach to those who have never heard that name Jesus. What else is worthwhile in this life? I have heard nothing better. 'Lord, send me!'" (S.A., 60).

In his final note to his wife Elizabeth, dated January 4 and found on the river beach where he died, Elliot wrote, "Our hopes are up but no sign of the 'neighbors' yet. Perhaps today is the day the Aucas will be reached….We're going down now, pistols, gifts, novelties in our pockets, prayer in our hearts. All for now. Your lover, Jim."

Jim Elliot's journal entry of October 28, 1949 is famous. Do not miss its context or you will miss a marvelous blessing. I will allow Jim's journal to speak for itself. No commentary will be needed.

October 27

Enjoyed much sweetness in the reading of the last months of Brainerd's life. How consonant are his thoughts to my own regarding the 'true and false religion of this late day.' Saw, in reading him, the value of these notations and was much encouraged to think of a life of godliness in the light of an early death....I have prayed for new men, fiery, reckless men, possessed of uncontrollably youthful passion — these lit by the Spirit of God. I have prayed for new words, explosive, direct, simple words. I have prayed for new miracles. Explaining old miracles will not do. If God is to be known as the God who does wonders in heaven and earth, then God must produce for this generation. Lord, fill preachers and preaching with Thy power. How long dare we go on without tears, without moral passions, hatred and love? Not long, I pray, Lord Jesus, not long....

October 28

One of the great blessings of heaven is the appreciation of heaven on earth — Ephesian truth. He is no fool who gives what he cannot keep to gain that which he cannot lose.

Jim Elliot said, "Our orders are: the gospel to every creature" (*Time*, 10). Because he believed this he said,

Nothing is too good to be: so believe, believe to see. In my own experience I have found that the most extravagant dreams of boyhood have not surpassed the great experience of being in the will of God, and I believe that nothing could be better. That is not to say that I do not want other things, and other ways of living, and other places to see, but in my right mind I know that my hopes and plans for myself could not be any better than He has arranged and fulfilled them. Thus may we all find it, and know the truth of the Word which says, 'He will be our guide even until death.'" (S.A., 196).

Jim did give up that which he could not keep to gain that which he could not lose. Now the question is before us: Will I? Will you? Oh God, give us more Jim Elliots that all the nations may give You glory!

*"S.A." is *Shadow of the Almighty* by Elisabeth Elliot.
"Journal" is *The Journal of Jim Elliot*, edited by Elisabeth Elliot.
See also *Through Gates of Splendor* by Elisabeth Elliot.

Conclusion

&

Real heros are in short supply in our day. You could almost say there is something of a famine in the land they are so few and far apart. Oh, how we need men and women we can truly look up to and admire. The church of the Lord Jesus Christ is no different in this regard. She needs heros and heroines who can encourage and inspire her to greater faithfulness and service to our Lord and King.

The author of Hebrews understood the importance of heros. After all, he was moved by the Holy Spirit to write Hebrews 11:1-40. Here we meet men and women who had great faith in our great God. Many of them, indeed most of them, were just regular ordinary persons in whom God did the supernatural and extraordinary. Verses 35-40 are especially powerful and meaningful when you reflect on the lives of the five missionaries and their spouses we have studied. Read what the inspired text says:

Others were tortured, not accepting deliverance, that they might obtain a better resurrection. Still others had trial of mockings and scourgings, yes, and of chains and imprisonment. They were stoned, they were sawn in two, were tempted, were slain with the sword. They wandered about in sheepskins and goatskins, being destitute, afflicted, tormented-of whom the world was not worthy. They wandered in deserts and mountains, in dens and caves of the earth. And all these, having obtained a good testimony through faith, did not receive the promise, God having provided something better for us, that they should not be made perfect apart from us.

Rightly added to the names of Abel, Enoch, Noah, Abraham, and Sarah in God's "Hall of Faith" are the Careys, Judsons and Elliots, Wallace and Moon. All of them suffered and experienced trials and the testing of their faith. Some were even martyred. Yet they persevered. They honored our Lord and He has honored them. They are a reminder that God can take our little and do a lot. He can take our weakness and show Himself strong. He can take a short life and have it make an impact for all of eternity. Jim Elliot said it so well: we are just "a bunch of nobodies trying to exalt Somebody." May God by His grace and for His glory multiply the "nobodies," who have as their life's passion a desire to exalt the "Somebody" whose name is Jesus. These five who changed the world have certainly changed me. It is my hope and prayer God will use them to do the same for you and in you as well. I promise you this: if He does you will not be disappointed.

Sola Dei Gloria